MW01257333

CONQUERING
CRISIS

Also by Admiral William H. McRaven

Make Your Bed: Little Things That Can Change Your Life ... and Maybe the World

Sea Stories: Tales from My Life in Special Operations

The Hero Code: Lessons Learned from Lives Well Lived

The Wisdom of the Bullfrog: Leadership Made Simple (But Not Easy)

ADMIRAL
WILLIAM H. McRAVEN
(U.S. Navy Retired)

CONQUERING CRISIS

TEN LESSONS TO LEARN
BEFORE YOU NEED THEM

GRAND
CENTRAL

New York Boston

Grand Central Publishing
Hachette Book Group
1290 Avenue of the Americas, New York, NY 10104
grandcentralpublishing.com
@grandcentralpub

First Edition: April 2025

Grand Central Publishing is a division of Hachette Book Group, Inc. The Grand Central Publishing name and logo is a registered trademark of Hachette Book Group, Inc.

The publisher is not responsible for websites (or their content) that are not owned by the publisher.

The Hachette Speakers Bureau provides a wide range of authors for speaking events. To find out more, go to hachettespeakersbureau.com or email HachetteSpeakers@hbgusa.com.

Grand Central Publishing books may be purchased in bulk for business, educational, or promotional use. For information, please contact your local bookseller or the Hachette Book Group Special Markets Department at special.markets@hbgusa.com.

Library of Congress Control Number: 2024047473

ISBNs: 9781538771747 (hardcover), 9781538774380 (signed hardcover), 9781538774397 (B&N signed hardcover), 9781538772676 (large print hardcover), 9781538771754 (ebook)

Printed in the United States of America

LSC-C

Printing 1, 2025

To my three grandchildren: William, Elise, and Catherine. As you grow up, always try to be honorable men and women, work hard to take care of your family and friends, never give up on your dreams, and remember how much Papa loves you!

CONTENTS

AUTHOR'S NOTE

The events in this book are as I remember them. Any inaccuracies in the stories are a result of the passage of time or my advancing age. I have used some literary license with the dialogue, but I believe the conversations accurately capture the spirit of the moment. While the dialogue in chapter 5, in Churchill's war rooms, is contrived, the individuals, the decisions they made, and the events leading up to the operations against the *Tirpitz* are part of historical record. Additionally, I have changed some of the names and locations out of concern for national security and personal privacy.

INTRODUCTION

Houston, Texas, 2017

I am not easily starstruck. Throughout my life I have had the good fortune to meet kings and presidents, sports heroes and Hollywood stars, billionaires and Nobel laureates. These great men and women from around the world each, in their own way, transcended the ordinary, the common. They were, each in their own way, special. But the man who stood before me at St. Martin's Episcopal Church stood alone and above all my other heroes.

Maybe it was growing up in the sixties that shaped my admiration for him. Maybe it was the crew cut I got so I could look just like him. Maybe it was because of my father, a hero to me, who idolized this man above many others. Maybe it was when the entire world was glued to their black-and-white TVs, and his voice was calm and reassuring—repeating the words, "Houston, we have a problem."

Or maybe it was seeing him portrayed by actor Tom Hanks in the movie *Apollo 13*. But, whatever it was, I was in awe.

Captain Jim Lovell, now in his late eighties and long forgotten by many Americans, smiled and reached out his hand in friendship.

"I'm Jim Lovell," he said.

"Yes sir," I responded. "I know exactly who you are."

Lovell along with Jack Swigert and Fred Haise were the crew of Apollo 13 when on April 13, 1970, on their way to the moon, an oxygen tank exploded in the service module. The explosion forced them to abandon the command module (CM) and move to the much smaller lunar module (LM). The LM had very limited resources, lacking sufficient power, water, and oxygen for the three astronauts.

Within hours, the temperature in the LM began to plummet. The carbon dioxide scrubber, designed for two men, was struggling to keep up. The astronauts were running out of oxygen. Communication back to Houston was spotty at best, requiring the use of backup systems during critical calls. To make matters worse, the crew had to plot an entirely new trajectory around the moon and then find a way to use the command module for reentry.

Over the course of the next six days, the world held its breath watching the astronauts of Apollo 13 and the remarkable team in Houston fight through problem after problem. Flight director Gene Kranz, the director for both the Mercury and Gemini programs, was a steady hand during the crisis and as determined as anyone to get Apollo 13 home safely. To Kranz, failure was not an option.

Jammed into the lunar module, the crew of Apollo 13 seemed doomed to die in space. But on the ground, the team at the Johnson Space Center refused to surrender to the inevitable. Kranz and the engineering team (EECOM) in Houston calculated every liter of oxygen, devising a way to use the materials onboard to build a carbon dioxide scrubber to keep the astronauts alive. The power was constantly monitored, communications were restricted; pilots on the ground ran through multiple simulations to calculate the correct reentry angle: Every problem was relentlessly attacked and reattacked until a solution could be found. As the crew approached reentry, the three astronauts left the lunar module and returned to the command module. The LM was jettisoned and, with a prayer to the Almighty, the final reentry burn was conducted. On April 17, 1970, three days after the explosion onboard the Apollo 13 spacecraft, the crew of Lovell, Swigert, and Haise returned safely to earth.

Every component of a crisis existed in the Apollo 13 recovery mission. The explosion of the oxygen tank was *unforeseen and unplanned for. Lives hung in the balance. Organizational reputations were at risk. Time was a critical factor. Resources were constrained. And the whole world happened to be watching.*

Leadership during a crisis is fundamentally different from running an organization day to day. I have seen many a good leader wither under the pressure of a crisis. That's not to say that the basics of leadership aren't important during an emergency—they are. As a strong leader, during a crisis you must continue to be ethical, work hard, be confident, communicate with your workforce, and have a plan to address the problem. But a crisis brings an added layer of difficulty. A crisis pushes the limits of your experience. It challenges your confidence. It strains your team's morale and stretches your organizational resources. It entices you to make decisions before you're ready. It forces you to take risks, and it exposes every flaw in your personality and your organizational culture. To effectively lead through a crisis, you need additional tools.

Throughout my forty years of leading large and small organizations, I encountered every manner of calamity imaginable: from the personal crisis of being fired from a SEAL team to a crisis of confidence when I lost a boat at sea; from failed hostage rescues, special operations' raids that went awry, air strikes that hit the wrong target, almost getting kicked out of Afghanistan to being threatened by members of Congress and publicly embarrassed in Texas when a major project I supported fell apart. But I survived each of these moments and continued to advance as a leader because I learned early on what actions must be taken to resolve the crisis quickly and come out with one's professional and personal reputation intact.

In my experience, there are five phases of a crisis. Depending on the circumstances, each phase will vary in length and intensity. The first step is always the *Assessment*. What's going on? How bad is the catastrophe? How will it affect my organization? Correctly assessing the situation is key to what follows. Next is the *Reporting* phase. As a leader, you will have to report to your boss, your clients, your workforce, and the public. Accuracy in reporting is essential. Never mislead any of your constituents. Then comes the *Containment* phase. This is the most complex, necessitating a balance of speed and caution. Rarely do leaders get this phase exactly right. But knowing a balance is required is crucial. The containment phase is about preventing the crisis from getting worse. It generally requires the maximum amount of resources, strategically placed. You must stop the crisis's momentum to get the situation in hand. Once contained, you must *Shape* the outcome in your favor. Now the momentum is on your side. Finally, you must *Manage* the crisis. This could be a long-term proposition and requires a thoughtful use of manpower and resources until the crisis is resolved.

Like *The Wisdom of the Bullfrog*, this book is a series of stories from my career and my life. Stories with lessons. Lessons that I hope will provide the reader concrete steps to take when engulfed in a crisis— recognizing the danger of first reports, learning to weaponize the truth, managing time constraints, communicating effectively, maintaining organizational morale and esprit de corps, finding the best advice, prioritizing your options, and, most important, solving the crisis. *Conquering Crisis* is not just about surviving a difficult time; it is about thriving in a crisis, coming out stronger both personally and organizationally. *Conquering Crisis* will provide you the tools you need to be a successful leader when the unexpected arises. Whether trapped on the far side of the moon or ensnared in a public relations nightmare, sooner or later, every leader experiences a crisis. Get ready now!

CHAPTER ONE

First Reports Are Always Wrong

Owing to the chaotic nature of a crisis, a leader should always be skeptical about first reports. They are invariably inaccurate or misleading.

---- ✶ ----

The first report is always wrong.

—NAPOLEON BONAPARTE

The black teletype clattered as the spool swung from left to right, printing up the latest report from Station X. Station X, better known as Bletchley Park, was the source of Ultra, the top secret intelligence the Allies gathered after cracking the German Enigma code. Ripping the report from the teletype, General Edwin Sibert scanned the paper and quickly tossed it into the stack with the other highly classified documents. There was nothing of interest today.

Sibert, an officer assigned to General Omar Bradley's 12th Army Group, was confident in his intelligence assessment about the supposed German buildup in the Ardennes Forest. On December 12, 1944, he issued a report to the division commanders saying, "Attrition is steadily sapping the strength of the German forces on the Western Front...and the crust of the German defense is thinner, more brittle and more vulnerable." Three days later, British general Bernard Montgomery echoed Sibert's analysis, reporting that Hitler's army was in such disarray that "he cannot stage major offensive operations." Montgomery was so confident in his assessment that he wagered a five-pound note with Eisenhower that the war would be over by Christmas, only ten days away.

Elsewhere on the American front lines, the army distributed *Guide to the Cities of Belgium* pamphlets that described Belgian cities as a "quiet place for weary troops." For those who couldn't get leave to visit the cities, Marlene Dietrich, one of the most famous actresses of her day, entertained them with a USO-style musical tour. And the unfortunate soldiers who had to move to the front lines were told, "It has been very quiet up here and your men will learn [about war] the easy way."

But, deep among the oak and pine trees of the Ardennes Forest, German colonel Otto Skorzeny, the scar-faced commando whose exploits were so famous he had earned the title "the most dangerous man in Europe," was infiltrating behind Allied lines. His mission: to disrupt Allied troop movement, sabotage key supply points, and assassinate American and British leaders. Not far from Skorzeny's location, the German army had amassed seven Panzer divisions, thirteen infantry divisions, a thousand tanks and assault guns, and almost two thousand artillery pieces. And that was only the first wave of German troops. Behind them were another five divisions and two heavy brigades. All told, more than 200,000 German troops were preparing for an assault on the Allied front lines. Yet the intelligence coming into Allied headquarters remained optimistic. While Colonel Oscar Koch, Patton's Third Army intelligence officer, was adamant that an attack by a large Panzer concentration was imminent, other Allied reports remained confident that "a sudden attack in the West may with some certainty be said to have lapsed." In Bastogne, not far from the front lines, VIII Corps headquarters issued a statement that said, "Cloudy, snow, beginning around 1300. Visibility 2 miles. Nothing to report."

On the morning of December 16, 1944, the full might of the German attack was unleased on unsuspecting American and Allied soldiers. What would become known as the Battle of the Bulge had begun. However, even after the initial barrage of artillery, rockets, and cannon fire, the first reports remained inaccurate. In the early hours of the attack, most American generals still believed it was a feint and that the real thrust of a German advance would come from another direction. It was inconceivable to the Allies that the German army would attempt any large-scale assault in the dense forest and difficult terrain of the Ardennes.

When the initial reports began flooding into the 12th Army Group, they were so misleading that General Omar Bradley dismissed the German advances as a spoiling attack merely designed to stop the Allies' march toward the Rhine. Bradley was so confident his information was accurate that he joined Eisenhower that evening at the St. Germain-en-Laye villa to toast Eisenhower's recent appointment to a fifth star and play five rounds of bridge. Eisenhower would later say to General George Marshall, the chief of staff of the Army, that "all of us, without exception, were astonished."

As the conflicting reports continued to arrive, the Allies were slow to respond. Within hours, the Germans had advanced along a sixty-mile front, destroying American positions and executing those soldiers who stood in their way. The US 110th Infantry alone had 2,500 casualties during the initial German onslaught. Finally, the Allies realized the magnitude of the German assault and began to reinforce frontline positions, mobilizing more than 60,000 soldiers within forty-eight hours.

The Battle of the Bulge lasted almost thirty days, with 600,000 American soldiers engaged in combat; more than 100,000 were wounded, 19,246 killed in action, and more than 23,000 captured by the Germans. On the German side, more than 11,000 soldiers were killed and 34,000 wounded. The fight would put an end to the German army and Churchill would later say, "The Bulge is undoubtedly the greatest American battle of the war and will, I believe, be regarded as an ever-famous American victory."

None of this, however, acknowledges the fact that Allied intelligence failed the American soldier and that the first (and many subsequent) reports from the field were inaccurate and misleading, leading to a false sense of security and a delayed response at the battle's beginning.

In his remarkable book *The Guns at Last Light*, Pulitzer Prize–winning author Rick Atkinson says about the German buildup in the Ardennes, "To be sure, there were clues, omens, auguries. Just as surely, they were missed, ignored or explained away."

One might think that eighty years after the Battle of the Bulge, the US military would be better at gathering intelligence and even better still at ensuring first reports are exceptionally accurate. After all, we have satellites, high-altitude spy planes, drones, the ability to intercept telephone conversations and capture radio signals out of thin air. But the problem of first reports remains as challenging today as it did during World War II. In fact, the overabundance of information makes finding the *right* information more difficult than ever. Every leader should be cautious when evaluating first reports, and every leader should be equally careful about passing those reports to higher authority until the information is verified.

Chile, 1983, aboard the USS Spiegel Grove

In 1644, the French philosopher René Descartes published the *Principles of Philosophy*. In the book, Descartes attempts to prove the existence of God by arguing that man has the idea of a perfect being in his mind and therefore that idea could only have been embedded there by something perfect; the cause of the perfect idea is the perfect God himself. But Descartes also tries to show that man could be perfect if he carefully evaluated everything he saw and only made statements that were exacting in their language.

Descartes uses the example of a man in the desert who sees a building on the horizon. At first, owing to the distance, he believes the structure is round. But as the man gets closer, he sees that the building has four sides. It is not round, it is square. Descartes goes on to explain that man's imperfection is a result of his speaking before he has all the facts. I wish I had read Descartes before my first deployment as a SEAL platoon commander.

"Lieutenant McRaven to the bridge. Lieutenant McRaven to the bridge."

The loudspeaker aboard the USS *Spiegel Grove* blared throughout the ship, echoing off the steel bulkheads and reverberating across my small stateroom.

Ensign George Coleman, my assistant platoon commander, rolled his eyes and shook his head, his blond hair flopping back and forth.

"This can't be good news," he said.

Hopping out of my rack, I grabbed my notebook, straightened my uniform, and rushed out the door. I knew that Commander Bob Sumpter, the skipper of the *Spiegel Grove*, would expect me standing at attention within minutes of the announcement. Sumpter was not a big fan of Navy SEALs. Somewhere in his past the SEALs had done him wrong, and he seemed to resent everything about me and my SEAL platoon. It had been a rocky relationship since we started predeployment training and now, two months into a South America trip, things were no better off.

I two-stepped it up the ladder, opened the door to the bridge, and quickly made my way over to the captain's chair where Sumpter was sitting. Sumpter was known as "Screaming Bob," for his propensity to yell at his officers and senior enlisted. I was not exempt from his temper. Medium built, with a bushy mustache, a full head of hair, and a cigarette always in his hand, Sumpter was an old-world sailor, who believed in the infallibility and omnipotence of the commanding officer. If the Navy had put him in charge, then the Navy knew he was superior to everyone else on the ship.

"Yes, sir, you wanted to see me," I said, coming to a modified attention.

His gaze was fixed on the shoreline some three miles away. Picking up his binoculars, he pointed toward land.

"There is a lot riding on our exercise tomorrow.

You know that, right?" he said without ever turning toward me.

"Yes, sir," I responded.

"The Chilean chief of naval operations will be aboard the ARG, and Admiral Johnson will be joining him as well."

Johnson was the senior officer of our four-ship Amphibious Ready Group (ARG) and Sumpter's boss.

"I want to make sure the amphibious landing goes flawlessly."

"Of course, sir."

"That means that you and your frogmen have to blow the obstacles right on time, and I don't want any problems with the locals."

As part of this amphibious landing exercise, our SEAL platoon, along with the Chilean frogmen, would land on the beach, swim out to the concrete obstacles placed in the surf zone, load the obstacles with demolition, and destroy them. However, we had been forewarned that the local Chilean villagers were not happy about the exercise, and we needed to take every precaution to prevent any civilian disturbance.

Sumpter put down the binoculars, swiveled in his chair, and gave me a stern look.

"Are we clear?" he asked in a booming voice.

"Crystal clear, sir," I said rather curtly.

Sumpter didn't like my tone.

"Are you sure?"

"Absolutely, sir. I will ensure the demo goes on time, and the locals will be happy we were there."

"I know the Chilean frogmen are in charge of this mission, but you report back to me as soon as the obstacles are blown. You got that?"

"Got it, sir."

Turning his chair back, he stared out at the water. "Very well. Carry on."

Surrounded by high hills on three sides, the cove where we were landing was crescent-shaped and extended for about a half mile. The wide, white sand beach reached 200 yards inland. The light surf gently lapped against the shore. It could not have been a more perfect landing zone.

I watched as ten members of my platoon, partnered with ten Chilean frogmen, swam twenty-pound haversacks out through the small waves. Diving down ten feet, they tied the C-4 explosives to the concrete obstacles, connected each haversack with detonation cord, and then reeled the cord back to the beach. For our part, this was not exactly standard frogman tactics.

Since World War II, Navy frogmen had been clearing the beaches of obstacles so that the marines or soldiers could land without getting trapped in the surf zone. Normally, we would have been dropped off by a high-speed boat, swam our demolition to the obstacles, loaded the obstacles, and then been picked up by the boat. But, owing to the need for this landing to go "flawlessly," the Chilean leadership had directed their frogmen to be a bit less tactical and more administrative.

Coleman and the rest of the platoon soon emerged from the water.

"We're all set, Bill," Coleman announced. "We can crank off the demo exactly at 1400."

"How much do we have in the water?" I asked

"Ten haversacks, so about two hundred pounds," Coleman answered.

"Well, that should make a nice boom."

Chilean lieutenant Manuel Rosario, who had joined us a few weeks earlier, was standing next to me. Over six feet tall, with jet-black hair and piercing dark eyes, he was incredibly charismatic, and he had a smile that could charm any woman in Chile, which he did quite often. He was a platoon commander in the Chilean SEALs, called the Buzos Tacticos, and was responsible for the outcome of this part of the exercise.

"Is that all we are going to detonate?" he asked.

"Two hundred pounds is a good charge," I responded.

Manuel laughed. "I have detonated two thousand pounds on this beach without a problem," he said, waving his hands theatrically.

Looking down the beach, I noticed some Chilean enlisted men building another demolition charge. A large one.

"What's that for?" I asked.

Manuel smiled. "We will link all the charges together. It will make for a great explosion."

"No, no, no," I said. "That's too much for this beach."

"Ridiculous." Manuel chuckled. "I have deto-nated three thousand pounds on this beach without a problem."

I cocked my head and gave Manuel a questioning look. It would probably be 4,000 pounds next time I asked.

Pulling Manuel aside, I pointed out the fact that the beach was crescent shaped with high hills, and a low cloud deck had rolled in, all of which would amplify the sound wave from the explosion.

Manuel was adamant. We would link the charges

together. He had been given instructions to make the explosion on the beach as dramatic as possible for the benefit of our senior brass.

Down the beach about 500 yards was a nice two-story home. If the sound wave was going to break any windows, it would be theirs. Offshore, the *Spiegel Grove* and the other ships were in position to launch. It was 1345. We would detonate the explosives, all 1,500 pounds, right on time.

Crouching behind a sand dune, Manuel gave the order, and I heard the yell, "Fire in the hole! Fire in the hole!"

My demo man, Petty Officer Steve Case, squeezed the clamor clacker to initiate the blasting cap. A high-pitched whir from the clacker was quickly followed by the roar of 1,500 pounds of explosives ripping across the beach. The blast from the charge reminded me of the old film footage of the first atomic explosion at the Trinity test site in Alamogordo; the sound wave rippling the men's clothes, their faces stretched by the pressure of the explosion, their eyes wide with fear or awe. For me, it was mainly fear—fear that the 1,500 pounds of explosive had overpressurized the beach and likely blown out all the windows in the house down the road. The residents would not be happy. Which meant Sumpter would not be happy either. This could be a long day.

"Whoa!" Manuel screamed joyfully. "I don't remember it being that loud."

I shook my head and shouted to one of my enlisted men. "Brownie, go check the house and make sure we didn't damage any windows."

Within a few minutes, Petty Officer Dave Brown returned smiling.

"It's all good, sir. The blast wave must have missed the house. All the windows are intact."

"Whew," Coleman sighed. "I thought for sure we had shattered every window in that house."

After checking the men to make sure everyone was okay, I turned to Manuel. "How about the village? Any reports of damage?"

Manuel had a radio with one of his men in the small, rural town about a quarter mile off the beach.

"My man says everything is fine," Manuel reported.

"Sir, it's Commander Sumpter on the radio," Coleman said, passing me the handset. "Everyone on the ship heard the explosion. He wants to make sure everything is okay."

I turned to Manuel one more time. He was back on the radio with his man in the town.

"Is everything okay?" I asked.

"Yes, yes, yes, yes," Manuel responded. "No problem at all. No problem at all."

Picking up the handset, I felt a sense of relief. The charge had gone exactly on time. All my men were safe. There was no news of damage, and the locals would be happy.

Sumpter was uncharacteristically gleeful with my report. He immediately relayed our success to both the Chilean admiral and Admiral Johnson. Minutes later, the Chilean admiral was on the radio congratulating Manuel. As per standard operating procedures, we also sent a naval message back to the ship detailing our actions ashore, noting with some satisfaction that it was a large charge, detonated on time, without incident. All we had to do now was enjoy the show.

Over the next hour, I lay back on a large sand dune and watched as the small flotilla of Mike Boats carrying the US and Chilean marines began to land. As the procession of boats continued, I noticed a police vehicle driving onto the beach. The policeman exited the truck and strolled casually over to talk with Manuel. After a few man-hugs, the two men began laughing and pointing back toward the village. From my perch on the sand dune, I could tell that Manuel was reenacting the giant explosion. This was followed by more laughter. Getting up, I walked over to meet with the officer. After introducing myself, I turned to Manuel.

"What's this all about?" I asked.

"Oh, it's nothing," Manuel demurred.

"What's nothing?" I asked, a bad feeling rising in the pit of my stomach.

Manuel now seemed very uncomfortable but tried to hide it with more laughter.

"Well, the officer says there may be some broken windows in the village."

"Okay, how bad is it?"

Manuel laughed again. "Oh, I don't think it's bad. Probably nothing worth reporting."

The officer, who didn't speak a word of English, just smiled as we talked.

"I would like to see it for myself," I said, more sternly now.

Manuel tried to deflect, but I was adamant. We hopped into the officer's truck and drove into the small village. As I passed by the first house, the feeling of dread became even deeper. The front window was cracked from top to bottom. The village of about 1,000 people encompassed several square miles of modest Chilean homes, and as I passed from street to street,

I saw that not a single window was left untouched. While no one was injured, every pane in every home, church, and municipal building was cracked. The energy from the blast wave had focused all its power in one direction—toward the town.

After a few hours of talking with the local officials and ensuring them that we, the US Navy, would take care of damages, I headed back to the *Spiegel Grove* to make my report in person.

Standing at attention in front of Sumpter, I gave him all the details. I explained that our initial assessment of the post-blast effects was incorrect. I accepted responsibility for the errant reporting and offered to talk with both admirals myself. To my surprise, Sumpter took the news with unusual grace. He relayed to me a story about when he was a young ensign and, as the engineering officer, had incorrectly reported a systems casualty in the engine room, causing the ship's commanding officer to return to port, only to find out that everything was fine. In a strange way, after we both admitted our respective mistakes, our relationship got stronger.

Over the next several months, Sumpter used our SEAL platoon in every possible exercise. He frequently lauded the great work we did, and on several occasions he personally congratulated me for our professionalism. I began to appreciate why the Navy put Bob Sumpter in charge. Like all leaders, he had made his mistakes along the way. But he had learned from those mistakes, and he knew that by passing on those lessons to the next generation of leaders, he would make the Navy a better service.

Twenty years later, as a SEAL admiral in combat, my special operations task force conducted hundreds of missions to capture or kill high-value Al Qaeda targets. But each time the report came in from the field that we "got him," I remained skeptical until I could verify all the facts. Sometimes my caution frustrated both my staff and my superiors, but I came to realize that first reports are almost always wrong. This is why the assessment phase of any crisis is critical. When a crisis explodes, the people on the ground are generally panicked, traumatized, or under so much burden to report that they get the facts wrong. A leader should remain skeptical, both about the good news and the bad. Pressure will build for you to report quickly. *Make no declarative statements early on.* Absolutes are almost always wrong. Take the time to be cautious. It will be time well spent.

In a Crisis

1. Be very skeptical of first reports. Take time to verify the facts.

2. Be cautious about making a declarative statement in the first communication up the chain or publicly.

3. Have a corporate procedure for evaluating the quality of the information that is received during the first hours of a crisis.

CHAPTER TWO

Have a Council of Colonels

In a crisis, having a team of trusted advisors is essential for success.

Where there is no
guidance, a people fall,
but in an abundance
of counselors there
is safety.

—PROVERBS 11:14

Washington, DC, 1962

The world was on the brink of nuclear war. On October 14, 1962, an American U-2 spy plane photographed Soviet missile bases under construction in Cuba, just ninety miles from the United States. President John Kennedy immediately convened his "Camelot Circle," a group of trusted men and women from diverse backgrounds with diverse perspectives. The Camelot Circle included Bobby Kennedy, the president's brother and US attorney general; Ted Sorensen, the president's speech writer and close advisor; Arthur Schlesinger Jr., a historian and special assistant; Sargent Shriver, the president's brother-in-law and director of the Peace Corps; Pierre Salinger, White House press secretary; and Evelyn Lincoln, the president's personal secretary and close advisor. For days, the Camelot Circle worked in secrecy, planning and orchestrating Kennedy's initial response.

As reporters began to sense something amiss at the White House, Kennedy went on television and addressed the American people. On October 22, 1962, broadcasting from the Oval Office and looking confident and strong, he defined the nuclear threat; outlined the actions he intended to take; appealed to the Soviets, the Cubans, and the international community; and he made it clear that "this is a difficult and dangerous effort on which we have set out…but the greatest danger of all would be to do nothing."

While many of Kennedy's decisions were the result of his interactions with the joint chiefs and his cabinet, the strategy, the actions, the speech, the Oval Office presentation, the communiqués, and the final resolution were all greatly influenced by the Camelot Circle. Schlesinger provided historical context for the crisis. Bobby Kennedy facilitated back-channel communications with the Soviets. Sorensen drafted the president's address to the public. Salinger managed Kennedy's image, both domestically and internationally. Shriver helped maintain the president's morale and composure during the crisis, and Lincoln coordinated all his meetings and logistical support. Six days later, on October 28, Soviet leader Nikita Khrushchev announced that the missile sites would be dismantled. The world moved back from the brink of nuclear war.

For Kennedy it was the Camelot Circle, for Franklin Roosevelt the Brain Trust, for Eisenhower the Gang of Eight, for Reagan the California Advisors, for Clinton the Kitchen Cabinet, for Obama the Chicago Advisors, and for every military leader embroiled in a crisis, they turned to their council of colonels for the best advice and the unvarnished truth.

Kabul, Afghanistan, 2008

As the Blackhawk helicopter crested the final hilltop, I could see the sprawling city of Kabul spread out before me. Thousands upon thousands of small sand-colored brick structures dotted the landscape, occasionally punctuated by a brightly painted mosque or a concrete high-rise.

I had returned to Afghanistan recently after being gone for the previous two years. I spent most of 2003 to 2006 in and out of the country helping lead our special operations task force. During those three years, I felt we made some real progress in dismantling the Taliban and Al Qaeda senior leadership. Every night our SEALs, Rangers, Air Force special tactics, and Army special operations warriors were taking the fight to the enemy. Flying into the remote mountains of the Hindu Kush, patrolling to the caves of Tora Bora, or driving into the deserts of Kandahar, wherever the enemy was hiding, we pursued them. I was incredibly proud of all that we had accomplished.

As the helo made its final approach into the landing zone, the city center passed several hundred feet below me. The changes in Kabul over the past two years were remarkable. It was bustling with activity. The dirt roads had been paved. The vehicle traffic was pleasantly congested. The markets were full, and people were everywhere. I couldn't help but smile. We were doing good.

That morning, I had requested a meeting with the US ambassador, William Wood. Ambassador Wood had a great reputation. A career foreign service officer, he had served as ambassador to Colombia—another challenging post—and had worked closely with the United Nations and NATO. I was eager to build a working relationship with the ambassador and to get his sense of how the war was going.

After landing, we hopped into a couple of armored vehicles and headed to the Green Zone and the US embassy. It was a short ride through the city. We passed through security first at the outer perimeter and then the marine guard post, before my chief of staff, Colonel Randy Copeland, and I headed up to the ambassador's office.

The embassy had been completely renovated back in 2005. The old, dilapidated buildings were replaced with a soaring three-story structure built in classic Afghan style with clean lines, large windows, and a sandstone exterior. Inside was a large open atrium with a wide steel and wooden staircase that led to the working spaces above.

The moment we entered the ambassador's office, I knew something was wrong. Wood was gracious but restrained. His deputy was equally aloof. The ambassador motioned us to the sitting area and offered us some tea. The meeting started innocently enough—some small talk about my enthusiasm at being back in Afghanistan and my excitement about working with the embassy—and then the conversation took a nasty turn. Without warning, Wood exploded.

"Your tactical successes are leading to strategic defeat in Afghanistan!" Wood was suddenly seething with anger.

"What?!" I replied, stunned by his comment.

Wood continued, his voice getting louder and his face redder. His deputy sank deeper into the couch and tried to avoid eye contact with me. Wood repeated over and over that our night raids, our "harassment" of the Afghan people, our ignorance of their culture, and our unilateral actions were eroding the popular support we needed to win.

"This has to stop!" he shouted.

I'd had enough.

"Now wait a damn minute," I said. Or words to that effect... "I have lost dozens of guys fighting this war. My soldiers go out every night against the most difficult targets in Afghanistan. The reason there is any security at all is because we are targeting the Taliban and AQ leadership."

I stood up and leaned in, my fist clenched, my face Irish red, and my temper out of control.

"Who the hell are you to question my guys? You're sitting here nice and cozy in your embassy while my soldiers are out every night risking their lives. Don't you ever, ever question my men's desire to win this war."

"I would never question your men's courage or their desire to win the war. But I am telling you again that your missions are leading to strategic defeat!"

I was speechless, and the anger inside me welled up to a breaking point.

We moved within inches of each other, face-to-face. The deputy got up off the couch.

"Let's all calm down now," his deputy pleaded.

I looked Wood directly in the eye.

"We're done here," I announced, grabbing my helmet bag. "Let's go, Randy."

Wood didn't say a word as I stormed out of the office.

I marched down the stairs, past the marine at Guard Post One, and got back into the armored vehicle.

Copeland jumped in beside me. "You okay, boss?" he asked.

"Yeah, I'm fine," I replied, gritting my teeth.

"Damn, I thought you were going to hit him."

I took a deep breath and realized how close I had come to hitting a US ambassador. What the hell was I thinking? Nothing about that meeting went well. How could he possibly think that our task force efforts were hurting the war? I thought we went to great lengths to ensure our tactical missions were supporting the war effort. I was certain we did. Absolutely certain. Positive…

As we boarded the helo and began the flight back

to Bagram, I started to calm down. The sound of the blades muffled every distraction and I replayed the ambassador's words over and over in my head. The more I thought, the more I wondered. *What if Wood was right? What if our tactical successes were leading to strategic failure on the battlefield? What if we were hurting the war effort?*

By the time I arrived back at camp, I knew what had to be done.

"I want all the task force leadership mustered in the briefing area in the next hour," I told Copeland.

"All the leaders?"

"All the SEAL squadron commanders, their senior NCOs, the Rangers leadership, and all my senior staff."

Randy Copeland had been with me long enough to read my body language. This was not the time to talk me off the ledge.

"Roger, sir," he responded.

An hour later all the leaders in the task force were assembled in the briefing room.

"They're ready, sir," Copeland said.

The briefing area was nothing more than a large plywood room with a few cafeteria-style tables, folding chairs, and several portable whiteboards. I could hear the muttering before I entered. No one knew why they had been called on such short notice, and Copeland wasn't talking.

"Attention on deck," one of the chief petty officers yelled as I entered.

"Have a seat, gents," I said.

For a moment I paced in front of the whiteboard gathering my thoughts.

"Gentlemen, I just came from the ambassador's office, and he told me that the Americans are losing this war..." I paused. "Because of us."

"What the...!"

The looks around the room mirrored my stunned expression in the ambassador's office.

"He tells me that our night raids and our targeted attacks are undermining his efforts here in Afghanistan. He says we are not keeping the local Afghan leadership apprised of our missions, and we are forcing the Afghans to turn away from US support."

"That's bullshit," someone yelled.

"Yeah!" came a chorus of denials.

My operations NCO, a seasoned Ranger sergeant major, stood up.

"Sir, we call the BSOs every time we are conducting an operation in their area. We tell them to notify the local Afghan leaders so there is no fratricide and no surprises."

"Every time," the chorus agreed.

"So, the battlespace owners and the Afghan leaders know exactly where we are going and who we are going after?" I asked. Before anyone could respond, I continued. "And they get a chance to approve or veto our missions?"

"Well, sir, we don't give them a veto and, well... we don't ask for their approval, but we do give them the grid coordinates of our ops so there's no fratricide."

The more we talked, the more leaders defended their position. *They were doing everything right. Everyone who needed to know about our operations was informed. There was nothing else we could or should do.*

They were all experienced operators, and I trusted them, but I also couldn't discount what the ambassador had said. *Were our tactical missions leading to strategic defeat? Where was ground truth?* Were we the problem or was the ambassador just misinformed? I dismissed the leadership team and returned to my office.

"Well, boss, what do you want to do?" asked Copeland.

Gazing down at the Joint Operations Center (JOC) from my office on the second floor, I could see the incredible team of dedicated men and women all working to make a difference in this war. They came from every service, every three-letter agency, every corner of the United States. They were the best of America's sons and daughters. *How could I question them?*

"Randy, I need a council of colonels and someone strong to lead them."

Copeland smiled. "Roger, sir. A Council of Colonels."

A Council of Colonels. It was an old Army term for a group of experienced men and women who wouldn't hesitate to speak truth to power. For thousands of years, leaders in a crisis would turn to this council for advice, knowing that the handpicked soldiers would do what was best for the organization regardless of the personal cost to them.

"I need a team who can review all our procedures, question all our operational practices, and tell me whether we are doing all the right things. A group of officers and enlisted who know our operations inside and out and who won't be intimidated by me or the SEALs or the Rangers or the Green Beret operators.

Most importantly, I need a strong officer to lead them."

"I know just the officer," Copeland responded. "You need Colonel Bill Ostlund. Ostlund was a battlespace owner up in Konar. He's a Ranger and one of the smartest guys I know. He also tells it like it is."

"Get him. And get him fast."

Ostlund showed up in my office the next day. A battle-hardened West Point graduate with multiple master's degrees and extensive special operations experience, Ostlund was exactly the man I needed.

"Bill, I need you to pull together a team of experienced officers and enlisted. I need to know whether the missions we are conducting are furthering the war effort or whether our lack of proper coordination is detrimental to the fight."

I could see by the look in Ostlund's eyes that he was already building his team. Later that day, he assembled his council to help him do a deep dive on the organization. All men who he knew wouldn't hesitate to tell the truth to the admiral.

Within twenty-four hours of beginning his investigation, Ostlund was knocking on my office door. He had an initial report in his hand.

"Well, Bill, what's your preliminary findings?"

Without hesitation, Ostlund said, "Sir, I think the ambassador is right. The night raids and the unilateral missions are infuriating the Afghans, and the BSOs aren't happy either. While the guys are in fact notifying the BSO's staffs and to some degree the local Afghan leaders, the level of coordination is could be much better. When I checked with the actual BSOs, the brigade commanders themselves, they didn't have full visibility about what we are doing, and they were really hacked off that they don't have a voice in our mission set. We will need to do some major restructuring, take a hard look at the merits of the night raids, and completely redo our coordination SOPs if we are going to get this right."

"All right," I said, mulling over his comments. "How long will it take you to develop a plan of action?"

"About a week, sir," Ostlund said.

Out of the corner of my eye, I could see Copeland, pen in hand, just waiting for my next sentence.

"Randy, get hold of the task force commander and tell him I want to stand down the group for the next seven days. No operations whatsoever."

"Sir, you don't mean *no operations,* do you?"

"That's exactly what I mean. Until we get this

situation squared away, no one will leave the wire. Is that clear?"

"Yes, sir."

It didn't take long before all the operational leaders were in my office begging me to reconsider. *Think of all the bad guys that will get away in the next week. What about the innocent people that might get killed if we don't do our operations? The operators are fit to be tied they are so damn mad.*

I amended my order to allow for in extremis operations, hostage rescues, imminent attacks, but nothing routine.

In the next week, Ostlund and his council of colonels provided me a road map for reorganizing the coordination efforts, as well as another plan for adjusting the SOPs to ensure everyone in the chain of command was notified. But implementing the plan was going to take longer. Pushback from the operators ensued, and before long the complaints grew louder.

Another week passed.

"How are we doing, Bill?" I asked Ostlund.

"Sir, we are making some progress, but the group isn't ready yet. There is a lot of resistance to this plan, but I am convinced it's the right thing to do."

By this time, I was getting pressure from the International Security Assistance Force (ISAF) commander to get the task force back in the field. I took a deep breath.

"All right. You get another week, and then I will have to start operations again."

"Got it, sir."

By the end of the third week, the resistance had subsided, and we began to implement the recommendations from the task force study. We placed a liaison officer who reported directly to the brigade commander in every battlespace owner headquarters. We also doubled our efforts at ISAF headquarters and NATO Special Operations Force headquarters. We gave the BSOs a veto to all our missions and, more importantly, we ensured that our operations were complementary to the work the conventional forces were doing on the ground. Next, we established an Afghan coordination cell in the task force headquarters and placed an Afghan general in charge. Every mission we conducted was reviewed by the Afghans to ensure our targets were legitimate. By week four, the group was back in operation across the country. Over the course of the next three years, the task force conducted thousands of operations, killing or capturing countless high-value individuals and providing greater security for all of Afghanistan.

Finding out the truth about your organization can be challenging at times, particularly during a crisis. People close to you have a natural tendency to defend the organization and their position within it. Additionally, large institutions can become subject to groupthink, herd mentality, consensus thinking, or any number of confirmation biases. No one wants to believe they are part of whatever may have caused a crisis. Getting a correct and unvarnished assessment of the situation, early on, will make the difference in how you address the problem. It's at times like these when a leader needs to have a council of trusted advisors: men and women who will not hesitate to question the organization, its leaders, or its practices. In a crisis, find your council of colonels.

In a Crisis

1. Use the existing chain of command and your established staff to provide you valuable insights on resolving the crisis, but don't hesitate to have a group of trusted advisors (your Council of Colonels) outside the C-suite or the usual circle that can give you the unvarnished truth about the organization and your leadership decisions.

2. While your Council of Colonels can be essential to your decision process, do not exclude others on your staff from being privy to the nature of the discussions.

3. Use the Council of Colonels sparingly. Resentment will come quickly if the Council of Colonels too often usurps the normal staffing process.

CHAPTER THREE

*Bad News Doesn't Get
Better with Age*

*Delaying a painful truth never makes a situation
easier. The sooner you inform your boss about a
crisis, the quicker you can resolve it.*

---- ✹ ----

Bad news isn't wine. It doesn't improve with age.

—GENERAL COLIN POWELL

Balad, Iraq, 2008

The Iraq village of Janaja was eerily quiet as the small patrol of Army Special Forces soldiers maneuvered their way through the back alley. A light show of crisscrossing lasers from the soldiers' M-4 rifles peeked into every dark corner and open window, visible only to those wearing night vision goggles. Intelligence indicated that the high-value individual (HVI) they were hunting was holed up behind the walls of one of the large family compounds squeezed in between the maze of smaller brick homes.

"Fifty meters ahead," came a hushed voice over the radio.

"Roger," came the equally hushed response.

"Hold here. Bring the breachers up."

From the rear of the long, winding formation, two men silently moved toward the front of the line, stopping to talk quietly with the young Army major leading the mission. The formation halted, and each soldier took up their field of fire, their lasers now on wide beam as the muzzles of their long guns swept across the high stone walls surrounding them.

In the back of the formation, a fifty-pound Belgian Malinois tugged on its leash, anxiously awaiting its handler's command to attack. The radio squelched again.

"Move out."

As the formation approached the steel-gated entrance to the compound, the alley opened onto a broad cul-de-sac, exposing the soldiers to threats from all sides. Each man quickly moved into their stack position, ready to breach the gates and enter the compound.

High above the formation, an MQ-9 Predator drone peered down inside the walls.

In the command center, two hundred kilometers away, the Air Force sergeant controlling the Predator zoomed in.

"I've got movement inside the gate," he relayed to the ground commander.

"Roger. Is he armed?"

"Can't tell," came the reply.

"Move to breach. Move to breach," the major ordered.

Suddenly, a tall figure armed with an AK-47 emerged from an open doorway.

"Gun, gun, gun," came the yell.

"Gun, gun, gun," someone repeated.

In the command center, tiny figures on the flat-panel display moved rapidly, lasers darting from side to side. Over the radio the shouts of "Shots fired. Shots fired" rang out.

It was June 2008, and I had just arrived in Balad, Iraq, after taking command of the special operations unit from General Stan McChrystal. A newly promoted three-star admiral, I was the first naval officer to lead this organization. I had been the deputy commander for three years and thought the transition to commander was going smoothly.

The flight into Balad that night had been uneventful except for the usual spiral approach. Concern about surface-to-air missiles meant that every landing included a dramatic nose down, flaps down, hard, 360-degree dive from about 5,000 feet to wheels down. I always thought the pilots loved the opportunity to showcase their aerial skills, but to the passengers it was a bit unnerving. Nevertheless, we landed without incident, and I was quickly whisked away to a large concrete bunker that housed our command center. After several hours of initial briefings and reacquainting myself with the tactical situation on the ground, I headed to my room, hoping to get a few hours' sleep before the sun came up.

Being back at our headquarters seemed like coming home. While I had been gone for the past two years commanding Special Operations Command in Europe, I had spent most of the previous three years as McChrystal's deputy in and out of Iraq. However, the old tents and dilapidated trailers we used to live in during the early part of the war had been replaced by compartmented housing units, or CHUs. The CHU was a marked improvement to our old rooms and even had a small—very small—shower. After a quick shower, I hopped into bed. It was 0100 local time, and I just needed a few hours to recharge. Within minutes, I was asleep.

The banging on my door that woke me up thirty minutes later had an unmistakable sense of urgency.

"Yeah, yeah, yeah. Coming," I yelled, struggling out of bed. The banging persisted.

"I'm coming. I'm coming!"

I opened the door to find Lieutenant Colonel Sean Corrigan, my deputy operations officer, standing at the steps holding a classified document. Corrigan was an Army Green Beret officer assigned to my Special Forces unit. Small in stature, but tough as woodpecker lips, Corrigan had a huge intellect and a wry, cutting sense of humor.

"Evening, sir," he said as I tried to focus my attention.

"What's up, Sean?"

"Well, we have a bit of a crisis on our hands."

I waved Corrigan into my small room, and he laid out the classified report on my bed.

"Our operators were in Karbala tonight going after our target, Abu Walid, one of AQ's senior operatives in the area. As they approached the compound where we thought he was located, a man came out brandishing an AK-47. He pointed it at the force and they engaged him."

"And?" I said, waiting for the inevitable bad news.

"And...the man was just a security guard. But that's not the worst of it."

I shook my head, waiting for the other shoe to fall.

"The guard that was killed was Prime Minister al-Maliki's cousin, and the town where it happened was al-Maliki's hometown. The local Iraqis are furious."

Corrigan and I talked for a few more moments. As he started to leave, he looked me in the eye and said, "Welcome back to Iraq, sir!" I gave him a two-word response, and he just smiled. It was Iraq, after all. A crisis was a nightly event, but anytime an innocent person is killed, you carry that burden, and the crisis takes on an entirely different feeling. In wartime, things never seem to go as you planned, and when things go off the rails, they go off in a big way.

I looked at the clock. It was 0215 local. I put on my uniform, left my CHU, and headed to my office in the bunker. I knew what had to be done.

I picked up the red phone and pushed the button to call General Dave Petraeus, the four-star commander of the Multi-National Force—Iraq (MNF-I). Petraeus and I had crossed paths a few times during his initial tour in Iraq, but the encounters had not always been positive. As the commander of the 101st Airborne Division, Petraeus was responsible for securing Mosul, and his approach and my approach to getting the bad guys were not always in sync. Petraeus built strong relationships with the local Iraqi leaders and through those ties rendered the enemy ineffective. My unit conducted targeted raids against the enemy. These raids were effective in limiting the near-term threat, but in the long run, the Petraeus model was more enduring. His strategy in Mosul would become the template for how we engaged across Iraq.

One of Petraeus's aides answered the phone.

"Good evening," I said. "I'm Admiral Bill McRaven. I just took over for General McChrystal, and I need to talk to General Petraeus."

"Sir, it's two-thirty in the morning. General Petraeus is sleeping."

"I know. You need to wake him."

"Now?" came the incredulous response.

"Yes, now."

"Sir, can you tell me the nature of the issue?"

"Well, some of my soldiers just shot and killed one of Prime Minister al-Maliki's cousins. Needless to say, the locals aren't happy, and the sooner General Petraeus gets word of this, the sooner we can begin to address the issue."

"Oh, damn," came the response.

"Right. Now, can you please wake General Petraeus?"

"Right away, sir."

The line went quiet. A few moments later, I could hear footsteps approaching through the receiver.

"Yeah? What is it, Bill?"

"Sir, I'm sorry to wake you, but I didn't think this news could wait."

I proceeded to tell Petraeus the whole sordid story. He was not happy. The relationship between the multi-national forces and the Iraqis was always challenging, and Prime Minister Nouri al-Maliki was a difficult ally to work with. Anything that reflected poorly on al-Maliki's control of the occupation forces was politically radioactive. In the eyes of the Iraqi people, if al-Maliki couldn't stop the Americans from killing his cousin, how good a prime minister could he be?

After a tense few minutes of questioning, Petraeus leaped into crisis response mode.

"Okay, we need to notify Ambassador Crocker. Ask him to call al-Maliki. We need to get out a statement and accept responsibility. You need to begin an investigation as soon as possible, probably in concert with the Iraqis. We need to see what we can do for the dead man's family. And we need to get all this done before the sun comes up."

There was a pause on the line. I thought Petraeus was probably thinking about what else needed to be done.

"I know you just got into country, Bill, but this is a bad, bad situation."

"Yes, sir," I acknowledged, feeling that my first days in command had just gone terribly awry.

"But I'm glad you called and didn't wait until the morning. We need to get ahead of this, and every hour counts."

Petraeus hung up the phone, and we both got to work trying to do damage control. By the morning, al-Maliki had been notified, we issued a statement accepting responsibility, we worked on getting reparations for the grieving family, and I initiated an investigation.

Over the next three years, Dave Petraeus and I would work side by side in Iraq and Afghanistan. He once told me that despite the awful start to my command tour, he trusted me because he knew I would keep him informed even when the news was bad. That's the thing about bad news. It really doesn't get any better with age. If you fail to notify your boss, if you fail to make the bad news public, if you fail to disclose *all* the unpleasant details, the crisis will get worse. You will lose the trust of your superiors. You will lose the trust of the public. And after you lose people's trust, every step you take is questioned.

Washington, DC, the Pentagon, 1986

I was dragging. The days in the Pentagon seemed to last forever. Only four months earlier, I had been at a SEAL team preparing for a daring raid against Muammar Gaddafi's oil refineries off the coast of Libya. Now I was stuck behind a desk doing staff work for the SEAL community. I told myself it was important work, and it was, but it was still paperwork. I longed to be back in my wetsuit, freezing from the cold water, exhausted from hours spent in my little submersible, being constantly harassed by my fellow frogmen and as happy as a Navy SEAL could be. Now, as a young lieutenant, I was writing point papers, making spreadsheets, delivering briefings—all to get the SEALs more beans, bullets, bodies, and buildings.

It was 1500 and, mercifully, time for my afternoon stroll to the snack bar at the intersection of the A-ring and corridor three. The small room hadn't been updated since the Pentagon was first built in 1947. From the kitchen, the smell of popcorn and greasy hamburgers filled the halls around the A-ring. I loved it. As I entered, I noticed a crowd of twenty folks gathered around the small television mounted in the upper corner of the room. In 1986, the only televisions in the Pentagon were in the snack bars and maybe the military command center. I'm not sure about the command center because, as a lowly lieutenant, I was never invited in.

Hovering around the screen was Commander Monty Matthews, the EOD officer who shared an office with me.

"What's going on?" I asked.

"Some marine in the White House has been selling weapons to the Iranians," he answered.

I shrugged.

"Okay, so what's the big deal?"

"Well, according to the news, we're not supposed to be giving weapons to the Iranians because of the Iraq–Iran war and the arms embargo."

I shrugged again.

"Does it say why this marine was selling arms to the Iranians?"

"Not clear at this point. The White House says it's investigating."

"Was this some marine general?"

"No, no. It's some lieutenant colonel named North. Oliver North."

I glanced at the television as a picture of a squared away marine officer dressed in his blue uniform flashed across the screen.

"There is no way some marine is selling arms to the Iranians without someone else in the White House knowing about it. Is there?" I asked.

"The White House denies they had any knowledge of the marine's actions."

"Maybe he's some marine that went rogue," I offered.

"Man, Reagan is not going to be happy about this," Matthews said.

In 1986, President Ronald Reagan was exactly the man Americans felt they needed in the White House. Tall, handsome, with the swagger of a Hollywood movie star and a knack for making Americans feel good; even his detractors had to admit he made the country look strong. His approval ratings were some of the highest in history for a second-term president.

By the following week, reports were circulating that Lieutenant Colonel Ollie North had sold weapons to the Iranians in an effort to use the proceeds to fund the Contra rebels fighting the pro-communist

Sandinistas in Nicaragua. Assigned to the National Security Council staff, North worked out of an office on the third floor of the Old Executive Office Building. He commanded his clandestine operation from that office, setting up accounts in Swiss banks to obscure the financial trail and then concealing the operations from Congress. While it seemed unbelievable that a mid-level military officer could coordinate these actions without the approval of the president, with each report, the White House continued to deflect any suspicion away from Reagan.

Around the Pentagon, military and civilians alike debated the topic. The president was too well respected for anyone to suspect that he was involved in what was being called the Iran-Contra Affair. His office had made it clear that all the fault for this scandal rested with North and two other individuals, National Security Advisor John Poindexter and his predecessor, Robert McFarlane. Also of interest to the Pentagon was a young woman named Fawn Hall, who worked in North's office. She was a former Department of Defense employee; reports said she conspired with Oliver North to shred key documents that would have implicated others in the White House. On TV, the dashing Ollie North and the attractive Fawn Hall made for even more sensational reporting, and stories of clandestine late-night shredding filled the airwaves.

Two weeks after the story first broke, President Ronald Reagan addressed the nation from the Oval Office, confirming that the US had sold arms to Iran, but he made no mention of the money being diverted to aid the Contras. A week later, when it was apparent that reporters were making the connection themselves, Reagan held another press conference. This time he admitted to the nexus between Iran and the Contras. But, he said, that was the end of the story.

As the White House continued to withhold information from the public, reporters dug even deeper. Something still didn't add up. There was always a belief that the sale of arms to the Iranians was motivated by more than just money for the Contras. At the time, Hezbollah, an Iranian proxy group, was holding American hostages in Lebanon, but it was against US policy to negotiate with terrorist organizations or those that supported them. In his first press conference, Reagan vehemently denied any connection between the sale of arms and the potential release of the hostages. Little by little, the truth was uncovered. Finally, on March 4, 1987, almost five months after the story first broke, Reagan again took to the airwaves and admitted that arms sale to the Iranians was all about getting the hostages released.

Public support for President Reagan dropped dramatically from around 63 percent in October 1986 to the low forties by March 1987. There were talks of impeachment and serious discussions on Capitol Hill about limiting executive power. It would be another five years before the scandal was finally resolved, when President George H.W. Bush pardoned the six individuals indicted in the case.

All indications suggest that if Reagan had been transparent about the sale of arms and the diversion of money to the Contras from the beginning, the public would have forgiven him. While his actions violated the Boland Amendment, which prohibited selling arms to the Contras, and US policy against negotiating with terrorists, his purpose was to obtain the release of the hostages. Unfortunately for Reagan, none of these clandestine efforts secured the release of a single hostage, but Americans can be very forgiving if the endgame is a noble one.

Additionally, by trying to control the narrative and concealing the truth, Reagan lost the trust of the American people. Because he was not forthcoming, the nation had to endure years of public hearings and congressional investigation. This scandal was a tale of deceit and cover-up, brought on by the fear of exposure. My experience has shown me that bad deeds will always be uncovered. It is better to own the problem and make the bad news public than to conceal the deed and hope it goes away. It never does.

Interestingly enough, had Reagan studied recent history, he would have seen that two of his predecessors, John Kennedy and Jimmy Carter, both came forward immediately after their own national security disasters—the aborted Bay of Pigs invasion for Kennedy and the failed Iranian hostage rescue for Carter. In both cases, the public appreciated the presidents accepting responsibility and viewed it as a sign of strong leadership and accountability.

A crisis magnifies every leadership decision, and the most important decision a leader can make is to get all the facts, as unsavory and salacious as they may be, in front of key decision makers and, quickly thereafter, the public. Then and only then can you act with a single-minded purpose to solve the problem at hand, rather than spending all your time suppressing the bad news. This reporting phase is often the most gut-wrenching because it exposes you and your organization to ridicule, but failing to get the bad news out front will only delay the inevitable, and the ridicule will quickly turn to contempt.

I left the Pentagon in the summer of 1988 and did not return to Washington, DC, until October 2001. After the attacks of 9/11, as a Navy SEAL captain with counterterrorism experience, I was assigned to the National Security Council staff. On my first day I was given a small office on the third floor of the Old Executive Office Building. There, in a room that had been completely remodeled by a former occupant, was an old paper shredder. I was told never to use it.

In a Crisis

1. Never delay getting bad news to your bosses.

2. Remember, tell the truth, the whole truth, and nothing but the truth. Delaying bad news or misrepresenting the truth will erode trust and credibility between you and your boss or you and the public.

3. Acknowledge the severity of the incident, accept responsibility, and have a plan for addressing the crisis.

CHAPTER FOUR

Weaponize the Truth

Be transparent in your actions to resolve a crisis. The truth can be a great weapon against misperception and distrust.

I am a firm believer
in the people. If given
the truth, they can be
depended upon to meet
any national crisis. The
great point is to bring
them the real facts.

—ABRAHAM LINCOLN

Bagram, Afghanistan, 2010

Z oom in, please," I asked.

"They are definitely armed," someone in the JOC announced.

Sitting on a wooden bench behind Colonel Erik Kurilla, the 75th Ranger Regimental commander, I could see fifteen heavily armed men walking in single file, occasionally stopping to check their surroundings.

"Sir, we have comms with the battlespace owner, and he has given approval to strike if we're certain the Afghans are armed," Kurilla said.

"Oh, they're armed all right," the JOC non-commissioned officer (NCO) muttered. "I see AKs, RPGs, and a mortar. These boys are loaded."

On the large screen, I watched as the Taliban fighters struggled to carry their weapons up a steep hill. Several minutes later, they reached its crest, and the fighter with the mortar tube began to set up his firing position. Less than a kilometer away was an unsuspecting Afghan National Security Force (ANSF) outpost. We had tried to notify the outpost through our Afghan liaison officer, but to no avail.

My soldiers manning the JOC had been observing the men for five days. Owing to our lack of high-definition optics and the spotty reception in the mountainous terrain, it had been difficult to determine if these were armed fighters or just farmers moving from one location to another. But, as the fighters moved to high ground near the outpost, our view improved, and their intent became clear.

Our JOC was manned by more than one hundred soldiers and civilians, each with a specific mission. There were intelligence analysts reviewing the classified and open-source information in an attempt to locate HVIs and identify any threats to US and Allied forces. There were the operations officers and NCOs helping develop the plans and the concepts of operations for the missions. There were Air Force officers and NCOs managing the fleet of fixed-wing and unmanned aerial vehicles. There were the Army helicopter pilots and warrant officers coordinating all the rotary wing support for the insertions and extractions. There were the fires guys orchestrating the artillery and the combat air patrols. There were the MEDEVAC guys working with the conventional and special operations helos to provide emergency medical support when someone on the battlefield was wounded. Finally, there were a host of logistics support personnel providing all the combat and non-combat supplies and equipment necessary for success. All told, there were between 100 and 150 people continually manning the JOC. Every tactical decision I made, and every decision made by one of the officers or NCOs, was documented in a running electronic log. This allowed us to conduct a thorough debrief at the end of every operation. When something went wrong, which was a daily occurrence, we worked hard to correct our mistakes and improve our process.

As the Taliban patrol stopped for one final break, Kurilla turned to me and nodded.

"Now?"

I looked at the formation one final time. It was clear that they were in the last stages of preparing for the attack.

"Now," I answered.

"Fires, are we ready?" Kurilla asked.

"Sir, Pred is standing by and in position," came the response.

"Roger, you have permission to launch," Kurilla said.

"Roger, I understand permission to launch."

There was a slight pause, and then over the loud-speaker came the report.

"Bombs away, bombs away!"

At the command, two GBU-38, 500-pound bombs were released from the MQ-9 Predator flying high overhead.

"Thirty seconds to impact."

"Roger, thirty seconds."

On the screen, fifteen Taliban fighters stood in a small circle unaware that they had only thirty seconds to live.

"Ten seconds to impact. Nine, eight, seven, six, five, four, three, two, one, impact!"

The screen suddenly billowed with fire and smoke as the bombs hit their target. A plume of dust and rocks shot skyward, sending a shock wave rolling across the mountaintop that shattered the tall pines standing in its path. It was several seconds before the smoke cleared. The bombs had done their job.

*   *   *

"Sir, they are at it again. The local press is ripping us apart. They say we killed a bunch of innocent farmers last night. The governor in Mazar-e Sharif is calling Karzai to complain. This is bullshit!"

My chief of staff, Colonel Randy Copeland, was not happy. Copeland was the quintessential Army colonel—supremely organized, tactically and strategically sound, cared about the troops, and a great leader—but he hated anything and everything that reflected badly on our task force.

"Is it the same two reporters?" I asked.

"Yes, sir. It's Kathy McMannon from the local Afghan News and Sayed Joya from the regional bureau. These two have been running these conspiracy theories for years now. They had spread rumors about us torturing and killing innocents on a nightly basis."

Copeland was furious, and I couldn't blame him. But they did get half of it right. We were a black ops task force working out of a top secret base, but in our defense, no one went to greater lengths to prevent innocent civilians from being killed. As for claims of torture, I thought I had squashed that story years earlier when I allowed the International Committee of the

Red Cross complete access to my base whenever they requested. But apparently not.

"Well, I know what we need to do," I said.

Copeland smiled.

"Are you going to call Karzai and ask him to intervene?"

"Not exactly," I replied.

"Are you going to get in touch with Amrullah Saleh and ask him to pay them a visit?"

Saleh was Karzai's head of the National Directorate of Security.

"Nope, not that either."

Copeland had that worried look on his face now.

"Do you want me to call the head of the ANSF and see if the military will have a talk with them?"

"Too heavy-handed," I replied.

"Okay, sir. I give up. What do you want to do?"

"I'm going to invite the reporters to our base and show them how we conduct operations."

"What?!" Copeland stuttered. "Sir, you can't do that! We can't give them access to the camp. What if they report what they see?"

"That's exactly what I hope they will do," I said.

Thirty years earlier, I watched a documentary on arms control and disarmament in which a US Air

Force general escorted a group of Soviet generals through a top secret nuclear site. At the time, the visit to a US nuclear site by Soviet officers was considered extremely risky. The public concern was that the Soviets would learn everything about how we planned and conducted nuclear strikes. But the purpose of the visit was to build trust between the Soviets and the Americans as we attempted to implement the Strategic Arms Reduction Treaty (START). The transparency shown by the Americans became the cornerstone for our bilateral agreement, and START developed into a mainstay of nuclear diplomacy for the next thirty years.

That night I called General Dave Petraeus, the commander of the ISAF, and told him my plan. I would ask the reporters to respect the off-the-record nature of the visit and not to divulge names, location, or specifics. But they could use the information to frame how they reported on US activities. Petraeus, who always had a deep appreciation for the power of the press, immediately approved my request to bring the two reporters to my top secret base.

It took several days to coordinate the visit, but finally the two reporters showed up at the gate outside the camp, near Bagram airfield.

"Good evening," I said, greeting them at the gate.

They both had that deer-in-the-headlights look. I could sense a little fear in their eyes. They believed their own conspiracy theories and probably thought I was going to throw them in some deep black hole and keep them there until the war was over.

As we walked from the gate to my office, I pointed out the mundane things on the camp. Here was the laundromat, the church; the gym was down the road a ways. Here is the motor pool. I play basketball every Sunday on that hoop attached to the garage. My jump shot still needs some work, but no one can stop my hook shot. They weren't amused, but as we continued, their anxiety lessened. This base didn't seem as nefarious as they imagined.

We proceeded upstairs into my office, where I offered them coffee and tea. After a few minutes of small talk, I opened the blinds on my internal window, and there stretched out below was the JOC. Their eyes widened as they gazed intently at the drone videos displayed on the massive screens.

"So," I started, "let me walk you through how we conduct a mission. First, we spend days, weeks, sometimes even months building the intelligence package to ensure we have the right target. This includes imagery analysis, signals intelligence, and human intelligence."

On one of the displays, my intelligence officer had projected a standard intel package.

I continued. "Then we use a Predator drone to observe the target until we are certain it's the right person. This may also take hours, days, or weeks."

The two reporters were glued to the window.

"On the JOC floor, we have Air Force targeteers that will do an extensive collateral damage assessment (CDE) to ensure we don't inadvertently kill any innocent civilians."

"But you have killed innocent civilians!" Joya said tersely.

"We have," I admitted. It was a painful admission, but our operations weren't perfect. Occasionally, when a high-value individual was barricaded in a compound and our troops were taking effective fire, we responded. Sometimes that resulted in civilian casualties.

"Our primary objective is to capture the HVI so we can question him. Killing the target is the last thing we want to do, but sometimes if the risk to my force is too great and the HVI is too much of a threat, then we will execute a Predator strike."

I spent the next forty-five minutes explaining

exactly how we ran our operations. After that, I spent another hour fielding questions from the two reporters. At the end of the meeting, I escorted them out to the main gate and thanked them for accepting my invitation. They were gracious but curt.

"Well, boss, how do you think it went?" Copeland asked.

"I think they were still suspicious. They probably believe we orchestrated the whole evening and only showed them what we wanted to. But I hope the visit will dispel some of their concerns."

By the next morning, I had my answer.

There were articles in both the local and regional papers talking broadly about their visit to my base. While one of the reporters spoke in glowing terms, the other reporter was a little less enthusiastic. However, over the course of the next two years, neither reporter wrote scathing stories about our troops and on several occasions, they even defended our actions, providing facts to the public that helped correct the record.

The truth can be a powerful weapon in helping to resolve most crises. When a crisis occurs, the detractors always believe it is a result of individual incompetence, organizational mismanagement, or C-suite lies and cover-ups. While this is occasionally true, and there are ample examples of all the above, for most good organizations a crisis is just an unforeseen event that overwhelms a company and requires decisive action to resolve it. If the public or your stockholders or your bosses believe that this is an isolated incident and that you are acting in good faith, then they are more likely to give you the maneuvering space to resolve the crisis. If, however, they believe you are misrepresenting the truth or, worse, outright lying, then their suspicions, and the questions that will ensue, will severely constrain your ability to take decisive action. In a crisis, take every action possible to demonstrate transparency, answer every difficult question, and showcase the truth. It is your best defense against the uninformed.

Pacific Ocean, fifty-six nautical miles southwest of Japan, 2017

"Bridge, CIC here."

"Go ahead."

"Bridge, I have a vessel bearing 015 at thirty thousand yards."

"Roger. What's her speed?"

"She's making about fourteen knots. Looks like a large container ship."

"Okay. Let me know if she changes course."

"Roger."

There were light swells off the southern coast of Japan on the night of June 17, 2017, as the USS *Fitzgerald*, a Navy destroyer, headed back to Yokosuka after several days at sea. The visibility was good with only scattered cloud cover. On the horizon, the running lights of several freighters and fishing vessels could be seen in the distance. The Combat Information Center (CIC) was tracking the vessels on the ship's AN/SPY-1 radar, one of the most sophisticated phased-array radars in the Navy's inventory.

"Bridge, CIC."

"Roger. Bridge here."

"Bridge, we've identified the large container ship. She is the ACX *Crystal*, a Filipino flagged vessel heading to Tokyo. The *Crystal* now bears 012 at twenty thousand yards."

"Roger, thanks."

The analog clock on the bridge of the *Fitzgerald* read 12:45 a.m. local time. Another report came twenty minutes later.

"Bridge. CIC. *Crystal* now bears 009 at ten thousand yards."

On the bridge someone muttered, "Ten thousand yards. That's getting pretty close."

The officer of the deck (OOD) nodded but stayed on course.

On the bow, the sailor standing watch could see both the port and starboard running lights of the *Crystal*. She was approaching head-on. *Should he notify the bridge? Surely they knew the ship was on a collision course. By this time the officer of the deck must have awakened the skipper. The captain would know what to do.*

Asleep in his quarters, the captain was resting soundly knowing that his night orders required the officer of the deck to wake him if another vessel was within 15,000 yards and on a constant bearing.

By 1:20 a.m. the distance between the ACX *Crystal* and the USS *Fitzgerald* had closed dramatically.

"Lieutenant, that ship's getting awful damn close!" someone yelled.

As the officers and crew looked out from the bridge, the bow of the *Crystal* was now visible. She was on a direct collision course with the *Fitzgerald*. *Someone needed to wake up the captain. Someone needed to sound the collision alarm.* Surely the *Crystal* must see that they are on a collision course. *Someone needed to take evasive action. No one did.*

Emblazoned on the starboard side of the container ship in large white letters on a black background were the words ACX *Crystal.* The name soared above the *Fitzgerald* bridge window as the *Crystal* plowed forward, unaware of an imminent collision.

"Left full rudder! Left full rudder!" the OOD screamed.

The helmsman immediately thrust the joystick on the control console hard to the left, but it was too late. At 1:30 a.m. on June 17, the ACX *Crystal*, a 729-foot-long, 30,000-ton container ship ripped through the starboard side of the *Fitzgerald*. Water came pouring through the hull, trapping seven of the crew inside the berthing area. Within minutes, the compartment was flooded, and there was no way out. The seven sailors inside all perished. As the flooding continued, the ship's crew responded, immediately initiating damage control measures and providing first aid to the injured, including the commanding officer, and stabilizing the ship to prevent even greater loss of life. After hours of battling the damage, the USS *Fitzgerald* and her crew limped back to Yokosuka. Hundreds of lives were forever changed, and seven sailors would never go to sea again.

An investigation determined that there were multiple failures in seamanship and poor decision-making on the part of the *Fitzgerald*'s crew. As a result, the commanding officer, the executive officer, and the command master chief were all relieved of their duties. It was the single greatest loss of life at sea since an explosion on board the USS *Iowa* in 1989 killed forty-seven sailors. Until...

Pacific Ocean, near the Straits of Malacca, east of Singapore, August 2017

"CIC, Bridge. We have a lot of contacts out there."

"Yes, ma'am. It *is* the Strait of Malacca," came the curt response from CIC. "We're tracking over forty contacts within fifteen thousand yards. They are all lined up ready to transit the straits."

"Well, just get me through this maze, and I will punch your liberty pass for Singapore."

"Consider it done."

It was August 21, 2017, only two months after the *Fitzgerald* collision. The USS *John S. McCain* was preparing to enter the Strait of Malacca and was just a few hours' steaming time from Singapore. The crew had only been at sea for forty-eight hours, but they were excited about the prospects of liberty in one the world's great cities.

"Bridge, CIC."

"Go."

"Officer of the deck, I have a contact bearing 210 degrees, ten thousand yards. It's the *ALNIC*, a Liberian flagged tanker."

"Roger," the OOD responded. "That's getting a little too close for comfort."

Grabbing the bridge-to-bridge handset, the OOD called the *ALNIC*.

"*ALNIC*, *ALNIC*. This is US warship on a bearing of 210 degrees. Do you have me on radar?"

There was no response.

"I say again, *ALNIC*, *ALNIC*, this is US warship, you are closing my position. Do you have a visual on my location?"

No response. Moments later, the *ALNIC* was at 5,000 yards and closing.

On the bridge of the *ALNIC*, the captain could see the *McCain*. Picking up his bridge-to-bridge radio, he tried to establish communications.

"Ship approaching my bow on a course of 210 degrees, this is the tanker *ALNIC*. Request you initiate evasive maneuvers."

There was no response. Over the radio the sounds of dozens of merchant vessels filled the airwaves, blocking out any attempt to make good communications.

"OOD, we're on a collision course," the helmsman shouted.

"All ahead full. Right full rudder! Right full rudder!" the young officer yelled.

"Roger. All ahead full! Right full rudder," came the response. But nothing happened.

"I said right full rudder!"

"I'm trying. I'm trying," the helmsman screamed.

The sun was still below the horizon, but the morning air was clear as the bow of the *ALNIC*, riding high in the water, tore through the port side of the USS *John S. McCain*.

In the portside berthing spaces, the *McCain* began to fill with water, and ten sailors struggled for their lives. Immediately, the crew went into action trying to save the lives of their shipmates and keep the *McCain* afloat. Unfortunately, they were unable to reach the trapped sailors in the berthing area, and all ten sailors died. However, through the actions of the crew, the

McCain stayed afloat and was able to make port at the naval base in Singapore.

In less than three months, two of the most tragic naval incidents in recent history had occurred in the Pacific, and the United States Navy was experiencing an existential crisis it had not felt in decades

On November 2, 2017, the chief of naval operations, Admiral John Richardson, stood before the American public and outlined in detail the Navy's failures. His report was raw, candid, and acknowledged every shortcoming.

"There was a failure to plan for safety," he said. "A failure to adhere to sound navigational practices. A failure to execute basic watch standing procedures. A failure to properly use available navigation tools. A failure to respond deliberately and effectively when in extremis of collision. A loss of situational awareness. A failure to follow the international rules of the road. And for the *McCain*, insufficient knowledge and proficiency of the ship's steering system." Richardson then continued to detail the Navy's plans to fix the problems. Later, during a hearing before the Senate Armed Services Committee chaired by the man whose name was on the back of the USS *John S. McCain*, Richardson said, "I own this!"

Every known detail of the collisions of the *Fitzgerald* and the *McCain* was reported to the public. Every failure was elaborated. Every poor decision was reviewed. Every name of everyone responsible was made public. Richardson even sent the report to all the allied Chiefs of Navy, his colleagues and peers. John Richardson understood that the only way out of a crisis is to ensure that the truth and transparency lead the way.

In a Crisis

1. Use truth and transparency through the crisis to show that you understand the problem and that you are taking concrete steps to resolve the issue. It may be uncomfortable, demoralizing to the organization, and personally embarrassing, but deception and opaqueness are a whole lot worse.

2. Stand in full view of the public eye, take the hard questions, accept the criticism, and answer truthfully. Get all the negative reporting behind you so you can begin to move forward.

3. If there are whistleblowers who generated the crisis, praise them for their courage. Any attempt to suppress criticism from within will only result in a public backlash.

CHAPTER FIVE

Move All Your Options Forward

In a crisis, your choice of actions may be constrained by a lack of information. Therefore, always have multiple options available and at the ready.

The wise man bridges
the gap by laying out
the path by means of
which he can get from
where he is to where
he wants to go.

—J. P. MORGAN

The War Rooms
London, February 1942

T he ceiling fan wobbled as it tried to dispel the thick cigar smoke that hung in the air. Winston Churchill, gripping a brass-handled walking stick, paced back and forth in front of the large nautical chart draped on the wall in front of him. At each turn of his short march, he tapped the chart with the tip of his cane, puffing and mumbling to himself. Seated around a long, rectangular conference table, officers of the Royal Navy, the army, and the air force watched in silence as the prime minister traipsed, deep in thought. They knew not to disturb him at this point.

"Charlie, this is just bloody dreadful. Awful!" Churchill said, his arm sweeping across the map. "If the *Tirpitz* breaks out of her harbor in Norway, she could destroy half of the Royal Navy. And without a navy, we will lose the war."

Admiral of the Fleet Sir Charles Forbes rose from his chair. He adjusted his monocle as he approached the chart. "Prime Minister, with all due respect, we have tried everything to stop her, but she seems almost invincible."

"Oh, bullocks! We said that of the *Bismarck* as well, but she's now at the bottom of the Denmark Strait!" Churchill bellowed, slapping his walking stick on the table.

"But only after four hundred direct hits and two torpedoes," Sir Charles snapped back. "And we lost five ships in the battle, and over a thousand men."

Churchill puffed even harder on his cigar, his face growing red with anger. Sir Charles, realizing his error in judgment, lowered his voice and pointed to a set of ships' blueprints on the adjoining wall.

"Sir, the Germans have learned from the mistakes of the *Bismarck*. The *Tirpitz* has more reinforced armor than any ship in history. She travels always in the company of four smaller battleships, the *Scharnhorst*, *Gneisenau*, *Scheer*, *Lützow*, and a pack of U-boats. And, when she is close enough to shore, the Germans protect her with a dozen or so fighters."

Churchill, pulling a pair of dark-rimmed glasses from his vest pocket, leaned toward the map and looked intently at a tiny dot deep in a fjord of Norway. "And why, why can't we bomb their little anchorage here in Kåfjord?" Churchill asked, thumping the map with his fist.

Sir Charles furrowed his brow and looked to the end of the long table. "Algie, you tell the PM why we can't just bomb the little anchorage."

Pushing his chair back from the table, Lord Algernon Portal, the marshal of the Royal Air Force, slid past the officers and approached the chart. Puffing on his Meerschaum pipe, he sidled up next to the prime minister and scrutinized the chart.

"Well, sir, the fact is the Jerries have surrounded Kåfjord with some of the most formidable air defenses we've ever seen. Ack-ack guns ring the entire basin," Portal said, pointing to several gun positions along the bluffs. "And there is a constant patrol of Luftwaffe fighters. My Lancasters have been making runs almost every night for the past several weeks, and the losses have been staggering." Stepping back from the chart, Lord Portal grabbed a photo of the *Tirpitz* harbored in Kåfjord. "Sir, the mountains around Kåfjord also make it nearly impossible to get a good bombing run in. Not only do the Lancasters have to fight their way through the Luftwaffe air support and past the ack-ack guns, but then they have to dive from ten thousand feet into this basin and release the bombs, at the precise angle, to get a good hit."

Sir Charles snatched the picture from Lord Portal and slammed it down in front of Churchill. "And Winston, even if they get a good hit, the damn ship is so heavily armored it would barely make a dent."

Churchill inched away from the wall, drew long and hard on his cigar, and turned to face the men sitting at the table. "Gentlemen. The whole strategy of the war turns at this period to this ship." He continued, waving the picture of the *Tirpitz* in front of the officers. "She is holding four times the number of British capital ships paralyzed, to say nothing of the two American battleships retained in the Atlantic. We can't even resupply the island with her roaming the seas. I regard this matter as of the highest urgency and importance."

He thumped the table with his cane. "You've given me nothing but bloody excuses. I need a plan. No, I need multiple plans. If the air raids aren't working, then let's attack the problem through other means."

The room of twenty senior officers fell silent. Finally, from the far end of the conference table, a tall, dark-haired naval officer rose to speak. "Prime

Minister, Combined Operations has a few plans that might suit your needs."

Resting his cane against the table, Churchill took a seat. Just a year earlier, he had established the Combined Operations Command and appointed Admiral of Fleet Lord Roger J. B. Keyes as its first director. Churchill ordered this unit to conduct commando operations throughout Europe, hoping that in response to the raids, the Germans would be forced to disperse their soldiers. But Churchill realized quickly that Keyes was the wrong man for the job. He was too risk averse and, consequently, Combined Operations had been ineffective at best. Within a year, he replaced Keyes with the man now speaking at the end of the table, Lord Louis Mountbatten, the First Earl of Burma and a cousin of the king. "Well, well. Don't just stand there, Dickie, show me what you have." Churchill said.

Mountbatten reached down, grabbed a large leather satchel at his side, and moved to the front of the table. He opened the briefcase, pulling out its contents and spreading several charts and photos in front of Churchill. "We are recommending two different approaches, PM. One, a direct attack on the *Tirpitz* at her anchorage in Norway and the other, a more indirect attack on the only dry dock in the world that she could use for repairs."

Churchill took another puff on his cigar and leaned over to examine the charts on the table.

Mountbatten continued. "Prime Minister, British military intelligence has learned through Enigma that the *Tirpitz* is experiencing some problems with her main engines, and just last month, the destroyer *Richardson* was able to damage her aft gun turret."

Shuffling through a stack of photos, Mountbatten singled out an aerial overview of a massive ship's dry dock, surrounded by German gun emplacements. Before he could speak, Churchill grabbed the picture and said, "I've seen this, Dickie! This is Saint-Nazaire."

"Yes, sir."

Returning to the nautical chart on the wall, Mountbatten pointed to the city of Saint-Nazaire, located in France on the Loire River, just six miles from the Atlantic.

"Saint-Nazaire has the largest dry dock in the world, and the only one big enough to accept the *Tirpitz*. Without the dry dock, any damage to the *Tirpitz*'s main propulsion, steering, or outer hull will put her out of action for the rest of the war. We don't have to sink her; we just have to deny her ability to get fixed."

"But then why in hell haven't we been bombing the dry dock?" Churchill asked.

"Oh, we have tried, sir," Lord Portal responded. "But the Jerries protect her from the air as though the Führer himself were there."

"It's not just the dry dock, PM." Mountbatten added. "Saint-Nazaire harbors almost the entire Normandy coast submarine fleet. The Germans have recently added fifteen new reinforced concrete sub pens."

Churchill rubbed his chin and harrumphed. "Okay Dickie, so what's this plan of yours?"

"This is the HMS *Campbeltown*," Mountbatten said, reaching for a picture of the British destroyer.

Churchill picked up the photo.

"It doesn't look like any British ship I've seen."

"It's not, sir," Mountbatten responded. "The Yanks were kind enough to loan us one of their old vessels."

Churchill twirled the cigar in his mouth as he admired the *Campbeltown*.

"We've made some nice little modifications to the vessel." Mountbatten smiled.

Churchill grinned as he took a closer look at the photo. "Well, old Dickie, you've turned her into a German torpedo boat!"

"Very good, PM," Mountbatten exclaimed. "In

fact, we have cut away two of her four boiler stacks, shortened the draft by two feet, and added eight Oerlikon gun positions. Additionally, we put a little extra armor on the sides to protect our lads."

"Protect them from what?" Churchill smiled deviously.

"Well, PM, the fact is we want to run this little German torpedo boat up the Loire River and ram her directly into the dry dock. We also plan to have over six hundred commandos aboard the *Campbeltown* and some smaller patrol boats. When the *Campbeltown* rams the dock, the commandos will storm ashore and attack other targets."

Churchill gazed closely at the picture of the dry dock. From the aerial photo, it dwarfed all other structures around it. Annotated on the glossy were several numbers. The dock was over 1100 feet long and 160 feet wide. Owing to the pressure required to hold the water, the sides of the dry dock were 35 feet thick and the two locks at the end measured 54 feet high. It was an engineering marvel and a formidable target. Churchill shook his head.

"I'd be surprised if even a direct blow from a ship the size of the *Campbeltown* could damage so large a dry dock."

Glancing around the room, Mountbatten debated whether to provide further details to the assembled group. But it might be his only chance to convince Churchill of the merits of the plan.

"Well, sir. We have a little surprise of our own."

Mountbatten slid another picture from his stack of photos.

"Oh my!" Churchill grinned looking at the photo. "This would definitely do the trick."

Mountbatten smiled. "It would indeed, sir."

"What else do you have up your sleeve, Dickie?"

Mountbatten pulled one final photo from his leather case. "Now, for a more direct approach," Mountbatten said, passing it to Churchill.

"Ah." Churchill grinned. "An X-Craft."

"Yes, PM," Mountbatten acknowledged. "These three-man submersibles carry two side charges, each with two tons of explosives. Enough demolition to sink the *Tirpitz* at her anchorage if we can get the X-Craft under her."

"And how do you intend to do that, Dickie?"

Mountbatten pulled another chart from his case, spreading it out on the table in front of him.

"We have six X-Craft that will be towed from Loch Cairnbawn in Scotland, across the North Sea to the entrance of Sørøy Sound in Norway. From there, the X-Craft will make their way up the fjord and into the harbor where the *Tirpitz* is anchored. If only one of the six makes the journey, that will be enough to destroy the battleship and free up the Royal Navy to own the seas."

Churchill leaned over and examined the charts closely.

"There are bloody minefields at the entrance to Sørøy Sound," Churchill said, pointing to the location on the chart.

"And submarine nets, PM," Mountbatten answered. "But both the minefields and the nets are designed to keep our big boys away, not the X-Craft."

Running his fingers over the chart, Churchill smiled.

"My God, Dickie, these are ingenious plans."

Turning to Lord Portal, Churchill said, "Algie, I want you to keep up the bombing efforts. If only one of our Tallboy bombs gets a direct hit, it will be worth all that we have sacrificed."

"Yes, of course, PM."

"But, Dickie, I want you, Combined Operations, and the Admiralty to run with both the attack on Saint-Nazaire and the X-Craft mission. We can leave nothing to chance. I have only one question, Dickie."

"What is that, PM?" Mountbatten asked.

"Who have you found crazy enough to lead these missions?"

England, May 1991

As I stepped off the train from London, I felt like I had gone back in time. The quaint little town near the Cotswolds had not dramatically changed in the past two hundred years. The streets were lined with small stone houses whose windowsills were adorned with flower-filled planters. Green shrubbery surrounded the entrance to every home. An old stone church anchored the center of town, and everywhere I went the people smiled and nodded pleasantly.

The two men I had come to visit were legends in the special operations world. Having studied them for the past year, I knew everything about their military careers.

Admiral Godfrey Place had been a twenty-two-year-old Royal Navy lieutenant when he commanded *X7* which, along with *X6* commanded by Lieutenant Don Cameron, were the only two minisubs to complete the transit up the fjord and strike at the *Tirpitz*.

For his actions on that mission, Place would receive the Victoria Cross, the United Kingdom's highest award for valor. Place would later leave the submarine force and join the Royal Air Force, where he saw action in Korea, for which he received the Saint George's Cross, the second highest award for valor.

Lieutenant Colonel Robert Montgomery had been the second in command of the demolition team for the raid on Saint-Nazaire. Montgomery had been responsible for Mountbatten's "little surprise." He and his team loaded the bow of the HMS *Campbeltown* with four and a half tons of demolition, intending to ram the dry dock and detonate the explosives.

Montgomery's home was my first stop. He and his wife were incredibly gracious, allowing me to spend the evening with them learning details about the mission that weren't in the history books. It had been almost fifty years since the raid, but time had not lessened Bob Montgomery's memory of that historic operation.

On March 26, 1942, what had been dubbed Operation Chariot got underway. The HMS *Campbeltown*, with an embarked commando force of three hundred, was accompanied by eighteen small patrol boats carrying another three hundred commandos. The plan was for the *Campbeltown* to ram the dry dock while the commandos rushed ashore, destroying the submarine pens and other key targets. At one point during its transit from the Atlantic Ocean toward Saint-Nazaire, the *Campbeltown* ran aground but eventually dislodged and continued up the river.

At 0120 hours, on the morning of March 27, a German coastal radar picked up the *Campbeltown* and subsequently challenged the British flotilla. Intelligence had provided the German code, but as it turned out, the code had changed just prior to the British flotilla launching from England.

The official British after-action review noted that "at this time we must have been recognized as definitely hostile as we were suddenly fired on heavily and the action became general. It is difficult to describe the full fury of the attack that was let loose from both sides [of the river], the air became one mass of red and green tracer traveling in all directions."

Montgomery was on the bridge of the *Campbeltown* when German shore guns opened up and killed the helmsman. As the ship slipped off course, Montgomery immediately took the helm and began to steer the destroyer toward the dry dock. "I remember thinking, 'I'm an Army officer; I have no idea how to steer this ship.'" For several moments, Montgomery kept the *Campbeltown* on course until a naval officer took over.

At precisely 0134 hours, only four minutes later than planned, the *Campbeltown* rammed the dry dock, achieving the main objective of the mission. The force of the collision crushed thirty-six feet of the *Campbeltown*'s bow and drove her up on to the steel gate of the dry dock a full twelve inches.

With the destroyer clearly lodged and the timer on the demolition activated, Montgomery and his crew rushed off the ship and began to attack the other critical nodes supporting the dry dock.

Unfortunately, the rest of Operation Chariot did not proceed as planned. The commandos on the patrol boats came under withering fire, and the commandos from the *Campbeltown* failed to destroy most of their targets ashore. In the end, of the 611 men on the raid, 169 were killed and 200 were captured. The remainder escaped. Bob Montgomery was captured and held as a POW until the end of the war. However, at 1030 hours the morning after the Saint-Nazaire raid, the four and a half tons of explosives erupted, destroying the Normandie dry dock. The main goal of Operation Chariot was achieved, and the British considered the mission a rousing success. But for Churchill, this one mission was not enough to guarantee victory against the *Tirpitz* onslaught.

By early 1943, the prime minister was getting impatient. He had planned multiple missions to destroy or disable the *Tirpitz*. Only Operation Chariot had been successful, but that still meant that the *Tirpitz* could steam into the North Sea and engage the Royal Navy. Churchill wrote to his chief of staff, General Hastings Lionel Ismay, "Have you given up all plans for doing anything to the *Tirpitz* while she is still in Trondhjem [Kaafiord]? We heard a lot of talk about it five months ago, which all petered out. At least four of five plans were under consideration. It is a terrible thing to think that this prize should be waiting and no one be able to think of a way of winning it."

Unbeknownst to Churchill, the efforts to sink the *Tirpitz* had not petered out. In fact, Godfrey Place and the other X-Craft crews had been training for eighteen months in preparation for the attack. Place recounted the mission to me in great detail during my visit to his home.

On September 11, 1943, six large submarines towing six X-Craft departed Loch Cairnbawn at intervals of two hours. The first four days of the transit were relatively uneventful, but the conditions inside the X-Craft were almost intolerable for the crew. Towed by larger submarines, the small X-Craft bobbed like fishing lures on the end of a long line. The minisubs oscillated underwater relentlessly, and the cramped quarters were damp and exceptionally cold. The X-Craft surfaced four or five times a day to allow the crew some relief. During the transit, two X-Craft were lost at sea when their towing lines broke. The crews and minisubs were never recovered.

By 2000 hours on September 20, the four remaining X-Craft maneuvered through the underwater minefields around Kåfjord. After several days of transit up the channel, only X6 and X7 arrived at the objective. X6, under the command of Don Cameron, struck first, dropping their charges beside the *Tirpitz*. Unfortunately, the X6 was disabled in the attack and forced to surface. Cameron and his crew were captured. As the explosive charge went off, X7, helmed by Place, was just approaching the *Tirpitz*. The charge rocked X7 and, according to Place, "left X7 a bit of a mess inside." Now badly damaged but not out of action, the X7 dropped her charges under the *Tirpitz* and surfaced. Like Cameron's crew, Place and his men were quickly captured. Place spent the remainder of the war in a POW camp. However, between the attacks by X7 and X6, the *Tirpitz* was so badly damaged that she never sailed again.

"Old Winston knew exactly what he was doing," Place told me that evening. "He wanted multiple options for destroying the *Tirpitz*. It was the only way he could be certain that success could be achieved. As for me and the crews of the X-Craft, we also knew that our success depended on having multiple X-Craft and multiple chances at destroying the target. We hoped at least one of us would get through."

Years later as I commanded countless high-profile special operations missions, I never forgot the lesson of having multiple options to attack a target or deal with an emerging crisis. While the missions to destroy the *Tirpitz* had long lead times, the basic principle still applies. Have several options and ensure they are readily available. Time is not always on your side.

Washington, DC, August 1, 1990
2020 Hours

The president of the United States, George H. W. Bush, sat on the examining table in the White House Medical Office. Having spent the afternoon hitting a bucket of golf balls, the president had a sore shoulder and he was getting some heat treatment. Suddenly, the door to the small office swung open and Brent Scowcroft, the president's national security advisor, and Richard Haass, the NSC's Middle East expert, burst in. The look on their faces said it all.

"Mr. President," Scowcroft began. "It looks very bad. Iraq may be about to invade Kuwait."

While there had been some rumors over the past few days that Saddam Hussein was moving troops toward Kuwait and preparing for an invasion, most analysts believed he was just posturing and trying to force the Kuwaitis' hand.

Bush got dressed and returned to his quarters. Within the hour another report arrived.

"They're across the border," Scowcroft reported.

For President George H. W. Bush, this was the first post–Cold War test of the new geopolitical paradigm, and it was the most significant event America had faced in decades. The Iraqi invasion of Kuwait had all the tenets of a major crisis. First, despite the rumors, the invasion by Saddam was unforeseen and therefore most government agencies had no plan for dealing with the attack. Lives of American citizens and our allies hung in the balance. The reputation of the United States, as the global leader, was at great risk. Time was a critical factor, owing to the speed at which the Iraqi army was moving into Kuwait. US resources were constrained by other commitments around the world, and as tends to happen during geopolitical confrontations, the whole world was watching.

President Bush, having been the director of the CIA, the ambassador to China, and the vice president, was arguably the most experienced foreign policy president in modern history. He was also aided in the crisis by Brent Scowcroft, an equally professional and experienced national security advisor.

At the onset of the invasion, it was unclear exactly what Saddam's intentions were. Without intelligence assets on the ground in Kuwait, making initial assessments were difficult at best. The reporting coming from Iraq and from our Arab allies was often inaccurate and confusing. In the first hour after the invasion, Scowcroft convened the Deputies Committee, the seconds-in-command of all the major federal departments. Scowcroft needed a clear picture of exactly what was happening. Additionally, he immediately dispatched ambassadors, envoys, and military leaders to capitals and locations around the world to gather a better understanding of the situation and to assess our allies' willingness to support US efforts against Saddam.

At the same time, in an initial attempt to contain further Iraqi advances, President Bush ordered warships, including the USS *Okinawa*, to head to the Persian Gulf along with a squadron of Air Force F-15 fighters. Early the next morning, August 2, the US ambassador to the United Nations, Tom Pickering, called for and received a unanimous vote 14–0 in favor of UN Security Council Resolution 660, condemning Iraq's aggression and demanding it withdraw from Kuwait. Bush also spent much of the morning of August 2 calling heads of state around the world to get their support for potential US action.

At 0800 hours, on August 2, the president convened his National Security Council. Scowcroft later opined that the first meeting was a bit chaotic owing to the lack of information. However, as the invasion began, the US military developed a rough plan that was presented to the NSC. General Colin Powell, the chairman of the Joint Chiefs, and General Norman Schwarzkopf, the commander of US Central Command, briefed the president on a variety of options including air strikes, naval bombardments, oil embargos, protection of the Saudi oil fields, and the possibility of a full-scale invasion. While the military was prepared to react quickly, not every agency saw this crisis in the same light.

In the book he co-authored with President Bush, *A World Transformed*, Brent Scowcroft admitted that he was appalled by the undertone of the discussion at this NSC meeting. He said, "There was a huge gap between those who saw what was happening as the major crisis of our time and those who treated it as the crisis du jour. The remarks tended to skip over the enormous stake the United States had in the situation, or the ramifications of the aggression on the emerging post-Cold War world."

Scowcroft and Bush were under no illusion as to the magnitude of this crisis. They knew that in order to contain Saddam's aggressive actions and shape the outcome of the crisis, they would need to use all levers of American power—diplomatic, economic, and military. In light of the fact that this crisis was occurring on the other side of the world, all their options needed to be moved as far forward as possible, as quickly as possible.

On August 7, 1990, President Bush ordered the deployment of US ground and air forces to Saudi Arabia to protect the country from potential invasion by Saddam. Additionally, several carrier battle groups and amphibious ready groups were subsequently deployed to the Persian Gulf. This was the beginning of Operation Desert Shield.

Over the course of the next several months, the president exercised all his possible options. Through intense diplomatic efforts, a coalition of the willing allies were assembled in Saudi Arabia. This force was prepared to defend the country or invade Iraq, as necessary. Economically, a global trade embargo was implemented as a consequence of UN Security Resolution 661, subsequently cutting off all financial support to Saddam's regime. The president also received bipartisan support from Congress for military action.

What was clear to President Bush and Brent Scowcroft was that Saddam's invasion of Kuwait was no mere *crisis du jour*. The implications of not handling the crisis effectively would have reverberated across the international community and affect US global leadership for decades to come. Bush also appreciated the need to have multiple options available to him, thereby maximizing his decision space. Decision space, broadly defined, is the range of actions or choices available to a leader. The last option the president wanted to exercise was a full-scale military invasion.

However, on January 17, 1991, after Saddam refused to heed repeated warnings to leave Kuwait, the United States and our coalition partners invaded Iraq.

Within a hundred hours of the ground invasion, the coalition freed Kuwait and defeated the Iraqi army. Desert Storm remains one of the finest examples of US power and influence in the twentieth century. Few major geopolitical crises have been handled with such expediency and professionalism.

The nature of any crisis, whether it's a long-drawn-out wartime scenario like the 1940s operations to destroy the *Tirpitz*, a rapidly evolving international crisis like Saddam's invasion of Kuwait in 1990, or a corporate failing that splashes across the front page of the *Wall Street Journal*—all require the leader to examine every possible option available to contain, shape, and manage the outcome of the situation. Additionally, as with the *Tirpitz* example, an indirect approach to solving the crisis may be a good alternative. The leader leaves no option unexamined in an attempt to move all their options as close to the crisis site as possible. George H. W. Bush immediately ordered carrier battle groups, F-15 squadrons, and infantry divisions into the Middle East, thereby allowing him multiple response options. Leaders deploy their executive leadership team (their version of ambassadors, envoys, and military leaders) to the areas of most concern and use their local onsite staff to provide insights they can't gather through other means. Each of these steps will allow a leader to get a better assessment of the situation and manage the crisis to a rapid and successful resolution.

In a Crisis

1. Push all your options as close to the crisis as possible. This will allow you to maintain your decision space and move quickly when necessary.

2. Move a trusted, competent professional to the crisis site as quickly as possible and be prepared to deploy your people to every location that might be affected by the crisis. This will allow you to stay abreast of events as they unfold.

3. Have a prerehearsed plan for rapidly mobilizing your people and your resources. The nature of the crisis may come as a surprise, but the speed of your response should not.

CHAPTER SIX

Trust the Second Law of Thermodynamics

Crises never get better through inaction.

The most difficult thing is the decision to act, the rest is merely tenacity.

—AMELIA EARHART

Austin, Texas, 2023

I paced slowly in front of my class of twenty-five graduate students.

"Anyone?" I asked, tapping the whiteboard with my marker.

Eyes darted from side to side. Some whispers, but no one responded.

"Come on," I pleaded. "Surely one of you law students, public policy wonks, or military officers knows the answer."

"Sorry, sir," replied one Army major. "I'm just a supply guy."

"So, there are no engineers in the group? No one who even took an engineering class?"

Finally, one brave student raised his hand.

"I think it has to do with entropy," he said.

"What about entropy?" I asked, tapping the board again.

"Uh...uh," he stammered.

"You got it. Come on!" I roared.

"Entropy increases over time?" he said without confidence.

"Okay, I'll take it," I responded, laughing.

"I'm sorry, Admiral, but what does entropy have to do with national security?" the major said.

"I'm so very glad you asked. So, the second law of thermodynamics says that in an isolated system, the total entropy can never decrease over time and that the natural process tends to move toward a state of maximum entropy."

The class still looked confused, but before I could continue, one of the students belted out, "Oh, entropy is chaos. You're saying unless something changes, the natural state moves toward chaos."

"Right you are." I smiled. "And while my analogy may be stretched a bit, my experience is crises don't get better over time. You must do something to keep the natural process from moving toward a maximum state of chaos."

I returned to the whiteboard. Grabbing a blue marker, I made an x-y axis with time on the horizontal axis and degree of difficulty on the vertical. With an upward sweeping stroke, I drew a curve that rose quickly over time.

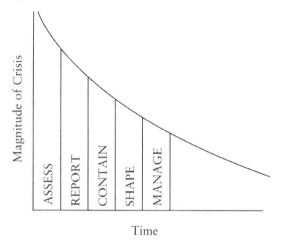

Time

"I call this the 'Strategic Decision Curve.' It isn't mathematically defendable," I said, "but what I've found is that when you fail to make a difficult decision early on, over time that decision gets harder because the crisis gets more complex. Unfortunately, most decision-makers fail to act quickly because the crisis hasn't evolved yet and they believe they have time to address the problem."

My class at the Lyndon B. Johnson School of Public Affairs was on national security decision-making. Over a three-week period, I put the students through five major scenarios and had them role-play members of the National Security Council. For the past several years, and long before COVID, we had a scenario on a pandemic spreading from Venezuela to the United States and eventually throughout the world.

Of course, the pandemic started small, but quickly spread. Before the lessons we learned from COVID, the students tended to react much too slowly, and decisions that could have thwarted the spread of our fictitious virus were delayed in hopes that things would get better. Having experienced COVID, students in later classes understood all too well what was at stake and acted more decisively.

What I have learned over my forty years of leading through crises, or just bad times, is that unless you take decisive action, things rarely get better.

Stuttgart, Germany, 2006

"He's just a cigarette smuggler," she said.

"He's the head of Al Qaeda in North Africa," I responded sharply.

The fluorescent lights inside the CIA compartmented facility seemed to flicker every time I raised my voice, and now they were flickering a lot.

"You guys have made him out to be a lot worse than he is," the CIA rep replied. "Yes, I know, he's got some ties to Al Qaeda, but it's all just local politics. It's good for his brand, but he's not a real threat."

For the past six months, I had been trying to get approval to strike a senior Al Qaeda leader in Algeria known as Mokhtar Belmokhtar (MBM). Having spent the previous three years as the deputy of a joint special operations task force chasing terrorists, I knew that MBM was coordinating AQ operations in North Africa and across the Maghreb—the swath of land that extends from Mauritania, across Morocco, Algeria, Tunisia, and into Libya. However, as the newly minted commander of Special Operations Command, Europe, I couldn't convince the local CIA representative in Germany that MBM was indeed a bad actor.

"What's it going to take to get your support?" I asked.

"What you're planning is crazy," she responded. "You want to fly an AC-130 gunship from England, across Europe, into Algeria, and kill MBM."

"Yep," I responded curtly. "That's exactly what I want to do."

"You'll never get the State Department or DOD to support this mission, and I can guarantee you, the Algerians won't be on board. They know MBM isn't a real threat to them."

She paused and rolled her eyes.

"But look. If you want to press ahead, I won't stop you."

That's all I was looking for. I thanked the woman and began to put my plan into play.

From the outside, MBM looked like a low-level threat, an Algerian jihadist known mainly for kidnapping and illicit activities. Often called "Mr. Marlboro" for his role in cigarette smuggling, he had taken to the mountains of Algeria in the nineties and joined the Salafist Group for Preaching and Combat. After the Salafist Group fell apart, he joined Al Qaeda in the Islamic Maghreb, where he funded a variety of failed jihadist operations. But while both the State and CIA didn't consider him a serious threat, my team of intelligence analysts and those at my previous command were convinced that if we didn't deal with him now, things would get worse.

* * *

"I don't know, Bill," the J3 said. "We're not used to doing these sorts of things here at EUCOM."

"I know, Bob, but I'm telling you if we don't get this guy soon, he's going to create real problems in North Africa."

"But he's not much of a problem now—is he?" the J2 asked.

"No," I conceded. "But we said the same thing about bin Laden in the nineties, and then Zarqawi, and Awlaki after 9/11."

"Okay, point taken."

Abu Musab al-Zarqawi had risen from relative obscurity to become the most infamous leader in Iraq. He was known for beheadings, market bombings, and kidnappings. Fortunately, right before my arrival in Europe, the US military put an end to Zarqawi's brutality. Anwar al-Awlaki was a little-known Muslim cleric in San Diego until he moved to Yemen and established Al Qaeda there. In 2006, it was still hard to convince people that Awlaki was dangerous. Time would prove those doubters wrong.

"Look. To be frank with you guys, I want your

support, but if I can't get it, I'm going to bring the request to General Craddock anyway."

Bob, the J3 operations officer, was a career naval officer who had known me for a long time, but the J2 intelligence officer was an Army officer who doubted my experience.

"You know that I will support you, Bill," Bob replied.

"All right," said the J2. "Count me in as well."

"Thanks, guys. I'll set up a meeting with Craddock and keep you both posted."

General John Craddock was the Supreme Allied Commander, Europe (SACEUR) in charge of all NATO forces and dual-hatted as the US European Commander (EUCOM). I had only briefly met Craddock, but my initial impression was good. He had a warfighter's heart. I was confident he would support the mission.

As expected, Craddock was not only supportive but also wildly enthusiastic. Within two weeks, we received approval from both the Departments of Defense and State. Now it was a matter of convincing the Algerian government that they should let us fly into their country and kill a known terrorist.

* * *

Sitting at a long, ornate conference table, the head of Algerian intelligence carefully reviewed the printed slides placed in front of him. Tall, with olive skin, dark hair, and a prominent mustache, the general rubbed his chin and stared at the graphic portrayal of the mission profile.

"So, you will not launch the mission from Algeria," he said in French.

"No," I responded, picking up just enough words from my high school French to understand his question.

"And there will be no attribution to the Algerian government?" he asked.

This time I turned to Lieutenant Colonel Fran Beaudette, my Special Forces commander and a fluent French speaker.

"He's asking if there will be any Algerian fingerprints on the mission," Beaudette said.

"Tell him only if the Algerian government wants credit."

Fran conveyed the message.

Looking at me, the general responded in broken English, "It would complicate things."

"I understand."

"You know that we do not think Belmokhtar is a real threat," he continued in French. "He has been operating in the region for years. He stirs things up occasionally, and we would like him dead, but why do you go to so much trouble?"

After translating the general's question, Beaudette turned to me.

"Sir?"

"Okay, Fran. Relay to the general that my experience in fighting terrorists tells me that if we don't address the problem now, it will only get worse. The longer MBM is allowed to continue his operations, the bolder he will get, and the bolder he gets, the worse it will be for Algeria."

Beaudette paused for a moment and then translated my words.

The general cocked his head to one side, a look of exasperation crossing his face. He hadn't wanted to meet with us in the first place. He had agreed only through a little State Department arm twisting.

"You Americans," he began, a surliness in his voice. "You ride in on your big white horse with your cowboy hat and you think you can solve all our problems. In the Arab world, we accept a little turmoil and generally the situation resolves itself. Not everything requires immediate action."

He pushed away the pages in front of him and looked me in the eye.

"We do not need your help," he said in English.

I smiled politely and said nothing.

Earlier in my career, I was stationed in the Philippines. I loved the Filipino people and the entire culture. Haggling in the marketplace was part of that culture. Whether you were buying a stick of gum or piece of furniture, the Filipinos loved to negotiate the price. I learned from haggling with the best Filipino vendors that you must look as though you don't care and be prepared to walk away from a deal.

I reached over and collected the papers that were in front of the general. He seemed surprised.

"Well, I thank you for your time, sir. I hope Belmokhtar doesn't cause you any more problems," I said, getting up from the table.

"Fran, let's go."

Beaudette quickly grabbed the remaining paper copies of the brief, and we began to leave. Around the room the other Algerian officers seemed concerned by my abrupt departure. *Who had offended whom? Why was the admiral leaving?*

"Un moment," the general said, his voice almost a whisper.

We continued toward the door.

"Un moment, s'il vous plait," he repeated, a bit louder.

"Oui?" I responded, somewhat curtly.

Looking at Beaudette, the general said, "Tell the admiral I will bring the issue to the president. But I make no guarantees he will agree."

While I understood the gist of his question, I looked to Beaudette to translate.

"Bon," I replied. "Tell the general that I look forward to hearing from the president, and the general can work through the embassy to get us his reply."

Now the ball was in my court again. I extended my hand and thanked the general and his team.

"I didn't think he was going to bite," Beaudette said as we left the building.

"He knows that if he passes on an opportunity to get MBM and later MBM does some spectacular attack, he will be held accountable. I'm his insurance policy."

"Do you think President Bouteflika will support the strike?"

"I have my doubts, but we should know within a week or two."

"Request permission to launch."

"Roger," I replied. "Launch the mission."

On the screen in my SOCEUR Joint Operations Center (JOC), I could see the small AC-130 icon begin to move. This was the final rehearsal before I requested approval from Craddock and the secretary of defense.

"That's pretty damn amazing, sir," the air ops officer said. "I've never seen a gunship take off loaded with that much fuel and ammunition."

It was true. We were exceeding the maximum takeoff weight for the aircraft. Colonel Brad Webb, the commander of the 352nd Special Operations Wing at RAF Mildenhall in the UK, needed Mother Air Force to approve the waiver just so we could launch the gunship. But Webb, one of the finest officers I worked with in my career, assured me that the gunship could take the load and get the mission done. I placed him in tactical command.

For the next eight hours, the AC-130 gunship flew in circles in the Atlantic to simulate the time of flight from the UK to southern Algeria, almost 2,700 miles.

"Sir, time on target ten minutes."

I put down my Rip-It energy drink and took my seat at the front of the JOC.

Minutes later I heard the call, "Weapons free. Target engaged."

Thirty seconds later came the follow-up call. "Target destroyed. Spooky RTB."

The man-sized target located on the range in the UK had been hit by six 105 mm Howitzer rounds. Nothing with flesh could have survived that strike. Eight hours later, the AC-130 returned to Mildenhall, and the rehearsal ended. I was ready to call Craddock and get the final approval.

"That's great news," Craddock said. "I'll call the SECDEF and have him get the president's approval. When do you anticipate conducting the mission?"

"Sir, we have the SIGINT team monitoring MBM's comms. As soon as we have a fix on him, I'll coordinate with the Algerians and order the strike. It could be one day, one week, or one month from now. It's just whenever MBM pops his head up. The crews will be ready to launch on a moment's notice."

After the call with Craddock, I contacted Brad Webb and had him put the crews on standby. Now it was a waiting game. MBM moved often to avoid being targeted by the Algerians. But there were times when he returned to a known sanctuary and stayed for almost a week. Invariably he would use his cell phone, and that was when we would get him.

"I know Bouteflika has given his approval," the ambassador said. "But I'm just telling you that they are not enthusiastic about this strike. They just don't think MBM is that big a deal, and they know if the Algerian people find out this was a US strike, it will make the government look bad."

"Yes, sir," I replied. "The problem is the Algerians just don't have the capability to get MBM, and my gut tells me that sooner or later, MBM is going to do something spectacular."

"That may be true, but they are betting that he won't last long in the mountains and that eventually someone else will kill him. The Algerians are a patient people."

"Well, sir, patience has never been my strong suit," I said. "And as soon as we get the trigger, I intend to launch."

The US ambassador to Algeria had been supportive

of the strike against MBM, but it was a difficult balance between his role in representing US interests and his need to stay on the Algerians' good side.

"I understand, Admiral. But you will be sure to give me a heads-up when you launch the mission."

There was always a concern, sometimes warranted, that we "special operations guys" would circumvent the State Department to get the job done. In my career, I never found that to be a winning formula. Keeping State abreast of all our activities was the only way to build trust.

"Absolutely, sir. I won't do anything without your knowledge and your approval."

"Thank you, Bill," he replied.

I thanked the ambassador for all his support and headed back home to get some rest. I hated the waiting game, but that's all we could do right now.

Days went by. Then weeks. Nothing heard from MBM. Finally, three weeks after the call with the ambassador, the signals intelligence team picked up MBM's location. They had identified his cell phone, but MBM himself had not made a call. It wasn't the trigger I was looking for. I needed confirmation that MBM was on the line. We waited a bit longer.

* * *

Once again, I was startled by the ring of the secure red phone. It was two a.m. when it woke me from my sleep.

"McRaven," I said, half awake.

"Sir, it's Mark," came the gruff voice of Colonel Mark Rosengard. Rosengard was the SOCEUR operations officer. A superb Army Green Beret officer, he had a wickedly dry sense of humor and a bluntness about him that I deeply respected. But I could tell by the tone of his voice that this was not good news.

"We've been f**ked," he said.

"All right, Mark. What's going on?"

"Sir, the f**king Algerians have tipped off MBM. He's making a run for it, and we don't know where he's going."

"Someone in the Algerian government tipped him off?" I asked.

"We don't know exactly who, but I just listened to the recording, and MBM knows our whole plan. He sounded terrified. Now the SIGINT team has lost his cell phone. We may never find him again."

Rosengard and I talked for a few more minutes. I called Bob at EUCOM and then General Craddock in Mons. At this point, there was nothing we could do. The following morning, I called the US embassy and asked them to relay my disappointment to the Algerians. The Algerians, of course, disavowed any knowledge of the call to MBM. Within a few days, we were told to stand down from the mission. It wasn't going to happen. I tried to reach out to the Algerians, but they wouldn't take my calls. Life got back to normal for me in Germany.

Over the course of the next ten years, MBM was responsible for the death of more than 150 people in four countries. He conducted numerous attacks in Niger, Mali, and Mauritania. In 2013, his group attacked the Tigantourine gas facility, a British Petroleum asset, in Algeria. The attack and subsequent rescue operations resulted in the death of thirty-nine hostages and twenty-nine militants. In March 2015, his group attacked a restaurant in Bamako, Mali, killing five people. Later that year, the group attacked a hotel in Bamako, killing twenty people. In January 2016, in Burkina Faso, he was responsible for another thirty deaths, and March of that year at a beach resort on the Ivory Coast, he killed another nineteen people. To this day, his whereabouts remain unknown.

In 2008, I left SOCEUR for another special operations command. For the next three years, I oversaw the capture or killing of hundreds of high-value targets. But all too often, when a terrorist threat appeared to be below the threshold for action, I was told to wait. There were some in the US government—all good, well-meaning, honorable people—who hoped the situation would resolve itself without decisive action. Decisive action always comes with risk. The risk that you might be wrong. The risk that you might bumble the operation. The risk that others might not approve. You are risking your personal reputation and the reputation of the organization you work for. These are all valid concerns. But the second law of thermodynamics has never been proven wrong. Left alone, the natural state of things moves toward maximum entropy. In a crisis, if you want to contain and shape the outcome, you will need to take decisive action to keep the situation from devolving into further chaos.

In a Crisis

1. You must take decisive steps to contain a crisis. Left alone, a crisis will get worse, not better.

2. The longer you delay in taking decisive action, the harder the decision and the action become.

3. There is always a difficult balance between rushing to failure and being slow to act. If you have to choose one or the other—act.

CHAPTER SEVEN

Don't Rush to Failure

In a crisis there is always the need to move quickly, but…don't move so fast that you outpace your planning, your preparation, your resources, or your strategy.

To lose patience is to
lose the battle.

—MAHATMA GANDHI

Monterey, California, Naval Postgraduate School, 1991

The man getting off the plane was younger looking than I expected. Having read about his exploits during the Korean War, Vietnam, and now his pivotal role in Operation Eagle Claw—the 1980 mission to rescue Americans held in Tehran—I assumed he would be balding or gray, slightly stooped, and maybe even a bit frail. But Major Dick Meadows, US Army, retired, was anything but frail. At sixty years old, with broad shoulders, a chiseled jaw, and sporting a crew cut, he still looked like he could run through a brick wall.

During the Korean War, Meadows falsified his birth record and joined the Army at age fifteen. His courage and leadership were so remarkable that he became one of the youngest sergeants in the history of the US Army. In Vietnam, his exploits were legendary. Working with the Military Assistance

Command, Vietnam—Studies and Observation Group (MACVSOG), a highly secretive special operations task force, he conducted countless behind-the-lines missions for which he received the Distinguished Service Cross, the second highest award for valor. He also played a crucial role in the famed 1970 Son Tay raid, an attempt to rescue American POWs from North Vietnam.

After Vietnam, he was recruited to be part of the elite Special Forces groups. It was during this time that Meadows went undercover into Iran as part of the mission to rescue fifty-two Americans held hostage by the Iranian regime. And this was the reason I had asked Dick Meadows to come to the Naval Postgraduate School (NPS) in Monterey, California.

As a student at NPS, I was working on my master's thesis, entitled "The Theory of Special Operations." I reviewed ten historical case studies to identify principles of special operations—those principles of war unique to commando missions. One of the case studies was Operation Eagle Claw. As one of the main planners, Dick Meadows had a critical role in the mission. I had extended an offer to him to come talk about the raid, and he had graciously accepted.

In April 1980, at the time of the rescue mission, I was a young SEAL lieutenant stationed at Subic Bay in the Philippines. When the hostages were taken in November 1979, the Navy began planning possible options to rescue the Americans. Little did we know that another unit had already been given the task. Under the tactical leadership of Colonel Charlie Beckwith, the plan was to airlift the Special Forces by C-130 from Oman to a remote landing zone inside Iran, code-named Desert One. At the same time, eight Marine RH-53D Sea Stallion helicopters would launch from the aircraft carrier USS *Nimitz*, fly to Desert One, and link up with the Special Forces operators. Once the linkup was complete, the helicopters would fly the force to Desert Two, a second staging area near Tehran. Finally, the operators would take trucks from Desert Two into downtown Tehran, assault the embassy, rescue the hostages, link up with the helos at a nearby soccer stadium, and fly to safety. Under any circumstances, this would have been an exceptionally challenging mission. However, to make matters worse, the timeline was compressed owing to threats against the hostages and a sense of political urgency from the Carter White House.

*　*　*

"Major Meadows, I'm Bill McRaven," I said, shaking his hand. "It's great to finally meet you."

He smiled, his big paw of a hand grasping mine.

"Well, it's a pleasure," he replied. "I thought to myself, anyone who puts this much effort into studying Eagle Claw is worth visiting."

Meadows and I had been corresponding for several months, and after a particularly intense period of questioning on my part, he jokingly yelled, "I surrender, I surrender. Let's just talk in person."

We picked up his bags and headed to a nearby pub to grab dinner. After a few beers, he began to talk about Eagle Claw. Unfortunately, the mission to rescue the hostages did not go as planned. After the helicopters lifted off from the USS *Nimitz*, they crossed into Iran and encountered a sandstorm. Three of the eight helos were forced to return to the carrier. The five remaining helos were late getting to Desert One, and by the time they arrived it was dark and the weather had deteriorated. The Special Forces operators had already arrived by C-130 and were waiting for the helicopters. During refueling operations at Desert One, one of the helos collided with a C-130, causing it to explode and killing eight men, three marines aboard the helo and five Air Force personnel aboard the airplane. The mission was aborted, and the ensuing fallout ended the presidency of Jimmy Carter and called into question the military's competence. It was clear to me that Dick Meadows still carried the mental scars from all that had gone wrong that day.

As the beers continued to flow, I got bolder in my questions, asking him about the shortfalls in the planning phase.

"We should have kept going with the rehearsal," Meadow said, the frustration still evident in his voice. "We should have done the rehearsal again and again and again if we needed to. Or come back the next day. We rushed everything."

I knew from studying the mission that Beckwith conducted a dress rehearsal at the Yuma Proving Grounds in Arizona. He felt the terrain closely matched that of the Desert One site in Iran. But, owing to a perceived sense of urgency, Beckwith never fully exercised all the aspects of the planned rescue.

"The colonel said the men were tired and needed a break," Meadows said, now getting angry remembering the conversation. "I begged him to extend the rehearsal another night, but he said we were running short of time."

Meadows took a sip of his beer, his thoughts somewhere in the desert of Yuma. "But we weren't running short of time. We could have used another two or three days to rehearse, but we rushed it. We rushed it," he repeated.

He downed the last of his beer. "But the colonel kept saying that the men were tired, and we would be just fine. I really respected Colonel Beckwith. He was a great soldier. What was I to do?" he said, looking at me for answers.

I had none.

After the disaster at Desert One, an investigation was conducted by Admiral James L. Holloway. The investigation lauded the incredible courage and sacrifice of all the soldiers, airman, and marines. And rightfully so. But it also concluded that there were massive failures in planning, coordination, training, equipment, command and control, and intelligence. Basically, every aspect of the operation was called into question. Most of the failures were compounded by a sense of urgency. When the planning began, the hostages had already been held captive for more than four months. Instead of immediately preparing for a possible military option after the hostages were taken, the White House attempted to secretly negotiate with the Iranian students before even considering a rescue mission. Had the White House planned in parallel, there would have been sufficient time for the military option to be prepared. Unfortunately, by March 1980, when the planning for Operation Eagle Claw began, the sense of urgency had heightened considerably, and Beckwith felt pressured to move quickly. Understandably so.

The next day at school, a more relaxed Dick Meadows gave a short presentation on Operation Eagle Claw and spent time with the students and the faculty. He was as humble, as gracious, and as professional as any soldier I had ever met. Meadows died four years later from leukemia, but his status as a legend in the special operations community never faded.

In 1711, Alexander Pope, an English poet, wrote a poem entitled "An Essay on Criticism." At the end of the second long stanza, Pope writes, "For fools rush in where angels fear to tread." It was a warning to those who take action before carefully considering the consequences. Two hundred years later, the American military adopted a version of Pope's famous saying and changed it to "Don't rush to failure," but the implications are just the same. If you rush through the planning and the preparation, then it's likely your actions will be flawed and result in failure.

Thirty years after my encounter with Dick Meadows, during the planning for the mission to get Osama bin Laden, I remembered those days in Monterey and Meadow's cautionary tale. Consequently, even though we had only three weeks to prepare, I ensured the SEAL team and the helicopter pilots rehearsed every aspect of the mission. Not once, not twice, but multiple times. We would take our time and do it right. Rushing the mission planning and execution would only get us in trouble. On May 1, 2011, Osama bin Laden was brought to justice, and I hoped that from beyond the grave, Major Dick Meadows was smiling.

Kabul, Afghanistan, August 2021

"What are we to do?" Mohammad yelled over the noise of the panicked crowd. "We can't get to the gate. The Americans have locked it."

"I know, Mohammed. I'm trying to find out. Just keep away from the crowds. I'll get back to you," I said.

"Thank you, Mr. Bill. Thank you."

I hung up the phone and called my contact at the State Department. Even though I was long retired from the military, I hoped someone could help.

Kabul was collapsing, and more than one hundred thirty thousand Afghans were trying to get into Hamid Karzai International Airport (HKIA) hoping for a ride out of the country on an American airplane.

In April of 2021, President Joe Biden announced that the United States would begin leaving Afghanistan on May 1 with the goal of a complete withdraw by September 11, 2024, twenty years after the attacks of 9/11. Over the course of the next three months, US troops left their combat outposts, their forward operating bases, and Bagram Airfield, the airbase with the largest concentration of American troops. However, there were still more than ninety thousand Afghan allies stranded in the country, allies who had helped the Americans during the past twenty years and who we had sworn to protect.

The US military leadership in Washington had been asking the Biden administration to begin evacuating these Afghans as early as April of that year, but owing to administrative red tape and political concerns, the administration waited. Now a crisis was upon them.

As the American presence on the ground evaporated, the Taliban saw an opportunity. On August 15, thousands of Taliban fighters swept into Kabul, and the government of President Ashraf Ghani collapsed, sending the country into turmoil. The administration immediately ordered Air Force C-17 cargo aircraft to fly to HKIA and begin emergency evacuation. But the initial effort was rushed and poorly executed. While the courage and the professionalism of the young airmen were without question, the chaotic scenes that followed were reminiscent of the downfall of Saigon fifty years earlier. The world watched in horror as desperate Afghans hung on to the wheels and the wings of the American aircraft as they tried to taxi and take off.

Within twenty-four hours, the 82nd Airborne Division landed in Kabul to coordinate the evacuation efforts, but the chaos continued as thousands more frightened Afghans stormed the outer walls of the airport and began to overwhelm the military contingent on the ground. Throughout all this unrest, the Taliban was a constant threat to the soldiers and the innocent Afghans trying to escape the collapse.

* * *

After a few failed attempts, I finally got through to my contact in the State Department.

"Sir, the Americans have closed Abbey Gate, and I don't know when they will reopen. It's pretty damn chaotic on the ground. But if you give me the names of your Afghans, I will put them on the list and hopefully when the gate reopens we can get them through."

"I'll text you the names, photos,and SIV information," I responded. "The father was an Afghan colonel who worked for me in Bagram. He's a good man, and if the Taliban find him, they will kill him."

"Yes, sir. I'll do everything I can to help."

I thanked the young foreign service officer and called Mohammad to give him the update.

It took another twenty-four hours before the gate opened.

"Breaking news!" came blaring across CNN. It was August 26, and a suicide bomber had detonated a device outside Abbey Gate. The exact number of deaths was unknown at the time. Within twenty-four hours, we learned that eleven marines, one Navy corpsman, and one soldier were killed along with more than 170 Afghans. That day, President Biden took to the airwaves and expressed his condolence for the loss of American and Afghan lives, but he remained committed to the withdrawal.

By August 31, 2021, just *two weeks* after the arrival of the 82nd Airborne Division, more than one hundred twenty thousand Afghans, American citizens, and our allies were evacuated from Kabul. It was one of the largest, most complex airlifts in history, and there is no other military in the world that could have conducted this mission with such effectiveness, professionalism, and personal courage. The American people should never forget that point. However, as impressive as this crisis response was, it was also, in my opinion, unnecessary. Had the administration accepted the military recommendation to begin an orderly evacuation in May or June or even July, it would have eliminated the need to rush the C-17s into Kabul in mid-August, thereby avoiding much of the chaos.

On September 15, 2021, Mohammad and his family arrived in the United States. They were the lucky ones. Thousands of our Afghan allies remained in the country under constant threat from the Taliban. While not all the chaos and failure of the evacuation can be attributed to hasty decisions and injudicious actions, the last-minute rush was certainly a contributing factor.

Almost seventy-five years earlier, the Soviet Union blocked all ground routes into West Berlin, attempting to force the United States and our western allies out of the city. Numbering more than two million people, the city had only a month's supply of food and water. As winter began to set in, the coal used to heat the homes was dwindling quickly, and the fear of starvation grew every day. Pictures of families trapped behind Soviet lines, malnourished children and struggling old people, were broadcast across the western world. Americans wanted action. We had just fought a world war, and now it appeared that our former ally, the Soviet Union, was carving up Europe. Something had to be done to help the beleaguered people in West Berlin.

Over the next year, more than 277,000 flights delivered around 2.3 million tons of supplies to the embattled city. At its peak, Allied planes were landing about one every thirty seconds, an astonishing feat that would be hard to match even today. What went unappreciated in the success of the airlift were the experienced officers who planned and executed the mission. Most notably, General William H. Tunner, who led the very successful India-China airlift over the Himalayas, the "Hump," during World War II. Tunner's experience precluded the need to rush the planning. He already understood what had to be done, and he executed it in a thoughtful, deliberate manner, even though the timeline was constrained. In their defense, the officials in the White House, the State Department, or most of the soldiers implementing the Kabul Airport evacuation had no similar experience to fall back on. The resulting evacuation, while showcasing the heroism and determination of the American soldier, also illuminated Washington's decision paralysis and the subsequent hasty operation.

My father, an old World War II fighter pilot, used to always caution me to "make a decision before you run out of runway." The saying had a very visual appeal to me. A crisis is much like a runway. You want to use all the available space you have to plan, prepare, and act before you reach a point where you have no room to maneuver. But, like a pilot speeding down the runway, knowing the takeoff point requires experience. If you lift off too early, you may not have the power to get into the air. If you start your acceleration too late, you may run out of runway before you can achieve flight. Nothing about a crisis is every easy, but take every advantage of the runway you have, and never rush to failure.

In a Crisis

1. Plan for the outcome you want to achieve.

2. Use all the decision space you have before taking action, but no more.

3. Time is your most perishable resource. Use it wisely.

CHAPTER EIGHT

Micromanagement Is Not an Ugly Word

During a crisis, you must make certain that those responsible for managing the outcome know precisely what you expect of them.

---✸---

Give attention to the
details and excellence
will come.

—OPRAH WINFREY

Virginia Beach, Virginia, 1985

The low-lying clouds obscured a full moon that was just peeking above the horizon. A cold February wind swept across the Chesapeake Bay, whitecaps masking the two frogmen who were swimming just fifteen feet below the USS *Spruance*.

As I was standing on the stern of the *Spruance*, the damp night air whipping across the bay was seeping into my bones. Zipping up my peacoat, I pulled my watch cap down over my ears and leaned over the railing looking for bubbles or motion below the water. Just two weeks earlier, I departed SEAL Team Four and arrived at SEAL Delivery Vehicle Team Two (SDVT-2) as the command's new operations officer. My job was to ensure the SDV platoons were fully trained and ready to deploy overseas.

The SEAL delivery vehicles were eighteen-foot-long, free-flooding, wet submersibles that could carry up to eight SEALs. Designed to be launched from either a submarine or a surface vessel, the SDVs could transit into enemy waters, sink a ship, or drop off SEALs on the beach. It was a unique maritime capability whose history dated back to the days of the World War II Italian frogmen and their manned torpedoes.

From the briefing I received earlier that evening, I knew that the SDV had bottomed out below the *Spruance* and two SEALs had emerged from its rear compartment carrying with them a large practice limpet mine. The SEALs would swim from the SDV to the hull of the *Spruance*, place the limpet mine on the keel, and then return to the SDV. Once back aboard, the SDV pilot would turn on the electric motor, being certain not to spin the screw too fast for fear of creating bubbles that could be seen by the "enemy" aboard the *Spruance*. Slowly, the pilot would maneuver his way from under the *Spruance*, back into the harbor, and then chart a course for home.

Walking the length of the stern from port to starboard and back again, I couldn't see a thing in the dark waters of the Norfolk harbor. It was a good night to be a frogman. An hour later, I received word from the safety boat that the SDV was clear of the harbor and heading home. Grabbing my small duffel bag, I thanked the crew of the *Spruance* for supporting the training mission and headed back home to Naval Amphibious Base Little Creek. Tomorrow would be another late night. Delta Platoon was getting ready to deploy to the Mediterranean, and after nine months of training, they had one final exercise that would determine if they were mission ready. The final exercise would also be my first opportunity to brief my new boss, the SDV Team Two commanding officer, on the platoon's readiness. A few hours of shut-eye, a few cups of coffee, and I would be raring to go.

Flipping to the next slide, I quickly outlined the concept of operations of the exercise for my boss.

"Sir, the SDV will launch from Little Creek, transit out past buoy one, turn on a course of 085 degrees for ten thousand yards, and the target vessel will be anchored approximately two miles off Fort Story. The SDV will have to float under the keel of the target vessel, unload their ordnance, and return undetected."

Rising from his chair, my boss, Commander Bob Mabry, strolled up to the screen, put on his glasses, and stared intently at the nautical chart in front of him. Mabry, who played linebacker in college and for a short time with the Vikings, still looked the part. Over six feet tall, with broad shoulders, powerful legs, and an eighteen-inch neck, his competitiveness was always on display. He wanted to win at everything, and if you were on his team, winning was the only acceptable outcome. Having served with Mabry on several occasions, I loved his intensity. But his professionalism and his experience as a SEAL were equally impressive. Unfortunately, a hit to his knee in the pros had never quite healed, and at forty-two years old, he was beginning to limp slightly.

"So, the target vessel is at anchor," Mabry said to no one in particular.

"Yes, sir," I responded.

Mabry knew that the hardest target for an SDV was a ship at anchor in deep water. On anchor, the ship would move with the current, making it hard for the SDV crew to approach it underwater. With the vessel in deep water, it also meant that the pilot couldn't bottom out the boat on the seabed and have the team swim the limpet to the keel. Everything about this exercise was challenging. That was the point. If Delta Platoon could attack a ship at anchor in deep water, they were ready for deployment, and a deployment during the Cold War always meant the possibility of secretly slipping into a Soviet harbor and sinking an enemy ship.

As I continued the briefing, Mabry abruptly stopped me mid-sentence.

"What are the currents like in the bay tonight?" he asked, his eyes staring at me over the glasses perched on his nose.

"Well, sir, I…"

"What time is moonrise?" he continued, stepping away from the screen and closer to me.

"Well, I think…"

"How about sunrise? This is a long dive. Will they be completed before the sun comes up?"

I glanced at the chart on the screen, hoping to see the times of sunrise and sunset. They weren't there.

"What is their backup plan if the SDV goes down? The mission says we must sink this ship by 0400. Is there a backup SDV? Who is the backup crew?"

The questions kept coming rapid-fire.

"Have you reviewed their escape and evasion plan? Does it seem realistic?"

Finally, Mabry took a breath, and I responded.

"Well, sir. I'm sure the platoon has all this information and a solid backup plan, but you know as the new operations officer I didn't want to micromanage their mission planning."

I felt so clever.

The term "micromanagement" had just entered the business vernacular. Micromanaging was considered derogatory because it implied that the leader of the organization was overly controlling and paid excessive attention to the small details. If you micromanaged, clearly you didn't trust your subordinates to do their jobs. Knowing that Mabry was exceedingly well read and loved to talk about business ventures, I felt certain he would appreciate my use of the word and my understanding of the concept.

"I'm sorry." Mabry paused, his jaw tightening slightly. "What did you say?"

Maybe I had misread the room.

"Sir, as the operations officer, I don't want to micromanage the platoon. I trust them to do their job, and I think they know what is expected of them."

"They know what is expected of them?" he said, shaking his head. "How do they know?" he asked pointedly. "Have you made it clear exactly what you expect?"

Now I was regretting having ever read the *Harvard Business Review.*

"Well, then, let me be clear. I want you to micromanage these guys. I want you to look into every detail of this mission. I want you to question every aspect of their plan. I want you to double-check their navigation, their communications, their insertion and extraction, their demolition, and their escape and evasion plan. And if there is anything you think can be done better, you should let them know precisely what you want done."

Mabry's tone softened. We had known each other a long time, and while he was significantly senior to me, we had become friends. In the years and decades to come, Bob Mabry would help me rise in the ranks. Today was a teaching moment.

"Look, Bill. This isn't about trusting the platoon. Delta is one of the finest platoons we have in the command. This is about making sure they understand your expectations. What I have found is that you need to micromanage people until they know precisely what you require of them. Then and only then can you loosen the reins. But if you're not clear about your expectations, then you shouldn't be surprised when they don't deliver."

He paused again and smiled. "This is just a training mission. But when the stuff hits the fan and you have a real crisis on your hands, you will have to be explicit in your directions. You will have to micromanage to get the result you expect."

Like a coach that just ripped one of his star players to make him better, Mabry slapped me on the back and told me to come back in two hours with the answers. Not surprisingly, when I checked with the platoon officers, there was some confusion about my guidance for the evening's mission. We cleared up the misconceptions, reviewed the planning, double-checked the details, and reported back to Mabry. That evening the mission went off without a hitch, and the platoon deployed to the Mediterranean later in the month. But Mabry's lesson on micromanagement stayed with me for the rest of my career. Every leader needs to ensure that their guidance is clear and unambiguous. During a crisis, this is even more important, as events tend to unfold rapidly and small errors in understanding and small errors in expectations can lead to disastrous results.

Austin, Texas, 2021

The Erwin Center was rocking. Five half-naked students with *TEXAS* painted across their chests screamed at the top of their lungs. Cheerleaders in burnt orange and white flipped backward across the floor. The band was playing the Texas fight song, and huddled along the sidelines were the two teams hoping for a spot in the NCAA tournament. The Longhorn basketball team was down by one point with seconds left to go. On the Jumbotron, Bevo, the Longhorn mascot, was snorting smoke out of his flaring nostrils and ripping apart the opponent's jersey. The noise meter was registering 110 decibels. I didn't think it was possible to get any louder, *but then it did*. A familiar face filled the big screen, and the crowd went wild. Wearing his signature tie-dyed T-shirt, basketball legend Bill Walton stretched out his six-foot-eleven-inch frame and changed into a shirt that read *Keep Austin Weird*. On the sidelines, the coach drew up the play. Moments later, the five men in Texas uniforms took the floor and, with military precision, executed a perfect play and won the game. Walton, a big smile crossing his face, flashed again on the screen. I could only imagine what he was thinking—*his former coach would have been proud of how the Longhorns performed*. If anyone understood the importance of executing every detail, exactly as planned, in the most difficult situations, it was the winner of ten national championships, Coach John Wooden.

In 2021, actor and former UCLA quarterback Mark Harmon presented me with a signed copy of Coach John Wooden's *Pyramid of Success*. Harmon and I had become friends through my association with the National Football Foundation, and Mark knew that I was a huge basketball fan. The Pyramid of Success was Wooden's approach to building championship teams, and this philosophy seemed to generate success both on the hardwood and in life.

As a young boy, I followed UCLA basketball with a passion. Watching Lew Alcindor (now Kareem Abdul-Jabbar) and Walton dominate the parquet floor was what I lived for. I knew the UCLA players were exceptional, but I had seen exceptional players fail to be exceptional teams. The common denominator to UCLA's success seemed to be Wooden. So what I studied in my youth was how Wooden coached.

John Wooden was born in Hall, Indiana, and from a very young age was a basketball junkie. In 1928, he went to Purdue University, where he was a point guard for the Boilermakers. At five foot ten, Wooden was known for his hustle, always diving for loose basketballs, but it was his passing and shooting that gained him national recognition. Three times he was named consensus All American, and in 1960 he was inducted into the Naismith Memorial Basketball Hall of Fame. After college Wooden played in the National Basketball League for several now-defunct teams. He was a master from the "charity stripe," hitting an incredible 134 straight free throws during a forty-six-game run. When World War II broke out, Wooden joined the Navy and served until 1946. But most Americans remember him as the *Wizard of Westwood,* the coach of the UCLA Bruins.

In 1948, Wooden was hired as the head coach. His first year, the Bruins had an amazing turnaround, winning the Pacific Coast Conference Southern Division Championship with a record of 22–7. At the time, these were the most wins in UCLA history. Over the next several years, Wooden took the Bruins to several NCAA Final Fours but couldn't win the championship. However, in 1965, a young freshman named Lew Alcindor joined the Bruins. Freshmen were not allowed to play that year, but by his sophomore year, Alcindor was the most dominant player in college basketball. In the ensuing three years, Wooden and the Bruins won three straight national championships. When Lew Alcindor graduated in 1967, the rest of college basketball drew a sigh of relief. Surely the Bruins couldn't repeat in 1968 without Lew Alcindor, *but they did*. In 1971, another high school prodigy named Bill Walton was recruited to join the Bruins. With Walton at center, the Bruins went on an eighty-eight-game winning streak, taking another two national championships in the process.

As a basketball junkie myself and a leader of the SEAL teams for thirty-seven years, I always wanted to know the secret of Wooden's success. I read most of Wooden's books, and clearly, he focused on building a culture that rewarded the good man. He believed that to be a good basketball player, you had to be a good person. Today, that approach may seem a bit quaint, but until someone bests Wooden's records, I contend it still matters.

In the Pyramid of Success, Wooden drives toward greatness by building upon a person's character. The bottom row of blocks includes such values as friendship, loyalty, and cooperation. The second row adds a dimension of initiative, alertness, and self-control. By the third row, Wooden begins to focus on the individual responsibilities that will make for a championship team. It was here that I found the nuggets of wisdom that I assert made Wooden's teams, and the teams

I later built, successful. The center block, the block that holds the entire pyramid together, is called skill. Wooden says that skill is "a knowledge of and the ability to properly execute the fundamentals. Be prepared. *Cover every detail.*" Cover every detail. It seems obvious, but so many times I see leaders leave the details to others. In an attempt not to be overly controlling or micromanaging, they fail to ensure their subordinates know exactly what is expected of them—particularly in a crisis. This failure to communicate the details, the exact expectations, often leads to confusion at the lower ranks and, subsequently, a poor outcome.

Wooden, of course, was a demanding coach. His practices were legendary. The plays were repeated again and again and again until Wooden felt the team knew precisely what was expected of them under every conceivable circumstance. When the game was on the line, with seconds left, it was this level of detail, this level of precision, this level of surgical execution, that made the difference between winning and losing.

By the time John Wooden retired in 1975, he had won ten national championships, received the coach of the year award seven times, and had a winning percentage of .804. No coach in college basketball history has ever come close to those records.

* * *

In 2011, I was given the task of overseeing the planning and conduct of Operation Neptune's Spear, the mission to get Osama bin Laden. For the operation, I "recruited" the finest team of SEALs and helicopter pilots I could find. They were all experienced combat veterans. There was no questioning their capability, but during the planning, I remembered my time at SDV Team Two and Commander Bob Mabry's counsel. Consequently, I carefully reviewed every aspect of the mission, from the planning phase to the rehearsals and finally to the execution of the mission on May 1, 2011. No detail was left unaddressed, and I made certain that my guidance to the SEALs and pilots was crystal clear.

When the first helicopter went down in bin Laden's courtyard, it looked like a crisis was unfolding. But on the ground and in my command center there was very little panic, because everyone knew exactly what was expected of them. For the past three weeks we had planned extensively for this possibility. I personally talked to all the helo crews and ensured they understood my directions. We rehearsed a downed helo contingency in the mission preparation. Multiple backup helos were loitering nearby in case we lost not just one but two aircraft. Additionally, as the commander of the mission, my ability to relay instructions directly to the men on the ground allowed me to quickly adjust to the changing situation. Micromanagement may still be considered an ugly word among business executives, but during contingency planning and when a crisis hits, make sure you provide the right level of oversight, communicating your intent with exactness and precision. It's the best way to ensure you can shape a successful outcome to a difficult situation.

In a Crisis

1. Check now to ensure your company's contingency planning is current. Preparation is the key.

2. At the beginning of a crisis, be exacting in your communications. Leave no doubt about precisely what you want done and how you intend to shape the outcome.

3. Monitor the crisis closely. As the conditions change, you may need to adjust your guidance to fit the situation on the ground.

CHAPTER NINE

Dictate the Tempo

Every crisis has a pace at which it unfolds. A leader must act quickly and decisively so the tempo of the crisis doesn't overwhelm your ability to respond effectively.

You can't let the
momentum of the
game dictate your
actions; you have to
stay in control and shift
it in your favor.

—SERENA WILLIAMS

Rome, 205 BCE, The Second Punic War

Fabius Maximus paced slowly in front of the Roman Senate, his long white toga adorned with a broad purple strip falling just short of the marbled floor. Tall, with a prominent nose, piercing gray eyes, and a fine square jaw, he was older than most of his fellow senators. A former general, Fabius had earned the nickname "The Delayer" for his tactic of wearing down the enemy in battle rather than confronting them directly.

"Hannibal has crossed the Alps, defeated us at Trebia, Trasimene, Cannae, and now he threatens Rome. If we do not stop him, what is left of the Roman empire will fall," Fabius remarked calmly.

From the floor of the Senate rose Marcus Claudius Marcellus, known as the "Sword of Rome" for his success on the battlefield.

"His army moves too quickly for us, Fabius. We

must do something to halt his advance and regain the tactical advantage."

"Is your nephew ready, Cornelius?" Fabius asked, turning toward an old man seated at the front of the Senate Council.

"He is ready, Fabius. His time is now," the old man answered.

"Very well. We shall make it so," Fabius responded.

Only twenty-five years old, Scipio Africanus was anointed as the leader of the Roman legions in 205 BCE. Already an experienced fighter, having served his father in several campaigns, Scipio was tasked by the Senate to stop the rapid advance of the Carthaginian army under the command of Hannibal Barca, the greatest general of the ancient world.

Over the course of the next several weeks, the young Scipio, in consultation with members of the Senate, devised a plan to swing the momentum of the war in Rome's favor. Reacting to Hannibal's tactical moves on the battlefield had been a strategic disaster. To gain the upper hand, the Roman generals knew they had to take action—action that would force Hannibal to slow his advance while at the same time gaining some ground for themselves. At this point, it was more important to slow the Carthaginian army and give time for the Romans to regroup than it was to advance the cause of Rome.

"It will work, Consul," the young Scipio argued. "It is the only way that we can gain an advantage without significant loss."

"It is a trickster's way," replied Senator Gaius Varro. "Real warriors should meet on the field of battle and let the best army win. And we are the best army."

"If we are the best, Gaius, then why is Hannibal soon to be at the gates of Rome?" Fabius asked.

Gaius grumbled at the retort.

Scipio, a look of determination in his eye, stood resolute in front of the 300 men seated before him.

"Gentlemen of the Senate, by crossing the sea and attacking Carthage directly, where we have a strong tactical advantage, it will force Hannibal to retreat from Roman soil and return to Africa to protect his homeland. Retreating will deplete his resources, weaken his morale, and force him to a battlefield of our choosing. A battlefield where we have the tactical advantage and where we can be victorious," Scipio said, his gaze firmly fixed on the senior senators.

"What will it take in terms of money and resources?" asked Tiberius Gracchus, one of the most prominent of the Roman senators.

"A great deal of Rome's treasure," answered Scipio. "But if we delay our actions any further, concerned about the short-term costs, all the resources in Rome will not stop Hannibal's advance."

An uncommon quiet came over the Senate, and only a few whispers could be heard among the great men of Rome.

Without warning, Fabius Maximus jumped to his feet and yelled, "I support Consul Scipio's plan, and I entreat all of you to do so as well."

From the Senate floor came a roar of approval, and the fortunes of Rome were about to change.

Over the course of the next year, Scipio raised and trained a new army and gathered the provisions, weapons, and equipment necessary for the campaign. In Sicily, a fleet of more than 125 ships were built and readied for sailing. The following year, with 30,000 Roman legions, Scipio sailed from Sicily to the shores of North Africa and laid siege to the city of Carthage, the home to Hannibal.

As predicted, the Carthaginian Senate immediately recalled Hannibal to North Africa, forcing him to abandon his Italian campaign. By the time Hannibal made it back to Carthage, his army was severely depleted. Scipio, seeing that he now had the advantage, engaged Hannibal at the Battle of Zama (in what is now Tunisia) and soundly defeated him. This brought an end to the Second Punic War, and Scipio returned to Rome a hero.

For more than fourteen years, the Romans had fought the Carthaginians from Spain, across the Alps, and onto the Italian peninsula, but were consistently defeated. Hannibal was the personification of an existential crisis: an enemy general who moved quickly, forcing the Romans to make hasty and imprudent decisions; a brilliant commander whose army overwhelmed the legions, draining their resources and destroying their morale; a visionary warrior who brought new and unforeseen tactics to the battlefield; and a ruthless, determined opponent who threatened the very center of Roman life. Hannibal dictated the tempo of the Italian campaign with his speed, his unconventional approach, and his masterful understanding of the Roman mind, and in doing so, kept the Romans off balance and constantly in distress.

Scipio knew that for the Romans to regain the advantage, they had to reclaim the operational tempo.

This meant slowing Hannibal's advance and then taking the initiative. Direct confrontation had failed, so Scipio took the indirect approach and forced Hannibal to retreat. Once the retreat started, the momentum shifted, and the Romans began to dictate the tempo and shape the outcome. Understanding how the tempo of crisis is unfolding, and how to shape it in your favor, is key to a successful resolution.

Indian Ocean, 1990, Aboard the USS Okinawa

Sitting in his chair on the flag bridge, Commodore Mike Coumatos, the Navy captain in charge of Amphibious Squadron Five, read the message quietly to himself. Beside him, his chief of staff, Commander John Smith, held a second copy in his hand.

"Well, this is embarrassing," Coumatos said.

"I should say so," Smith replied, shaking his head.

"You're telling me with all the warships we have in the Persian Gulf, the United States Navy can't stop one damn Iraqi cargo vessel?" Coumatos complained. "We've got destroyers firing across their bow and dragging cables trying to foul the rudder and we can't stop them?" he said again.

"It looks like the chairman isn't too happy either," Smith said.

"I would hope not," Coumatos said, stepping down from his chair. "This makes the US look both feckless and incompetent. Saddam Hussein is laughing at us. Did you see he's giving the captain of the Ibn Khaldun a medal for evading the Americans?"

"If I'm reading this message right, Chairman Powell wants us to stop the next Iraqi vessel heading to the Gulf and board and seize the ship," Smith said.

"Well, we have the only maritime interdiction capability in the region. It would make sense that the mission falls to us." Coumatos paused. "Ask Colonel Rhoads to join me in my stateroom and find McRaven."

Dressed in my khaki uniform, sweating from the heat of the Indian Ocean and a ship's AC unit that couldn't keep up, I scanned the photos spread across the small round table in the commodore's stateroom. Before me were black-and-white pictures of the Iraqi tanker *Amuriyah*. Nine hundred feet long with a seventy-two-foot freeboard, it was massive by any standard. The deck was covered with sixteen-inch fuel pipes running the length of the ship from the five-story pilot house all the way to the bow. What little space on the deck wasn't covered with fuel pipes was crowded with wires, poles, and large valves.

"What do we know about the crew?" asked Colonel John Rhoads.

Rhoads, a marine colonel with extensive combat time in Vietnam, was in charge of the Marine Expeditionary Force (Special Operations Capable). For the past eighteen months, the ARG and the Marine Expeditionary Unit (Special Operations Capable) (MEUSOC) had been working together as part of a routine deployment to the Western Pacific. In August 1990, that routine deployment quickly became a crisis response when Saddam Hussein invaded Kuwait, and we sailed through the Pacific Ocean on our way to the Persian Gulf.

"Sir, there are about thirty merchant seamen on the *Amuriyah*, but intel says they have been told to resist a boarding at all costs," I replied. "It is possible they have some small arms, but it's more likely they will resist using their ship's axes, sledgehammers, crowbars, and the like."

Coumatos picked up one of the more recent overhead photos and stared intently at the ship.

"It appears they have completely fouled the deck to prevent any sort of rappelling action by the SEALs or the marines."

"Yes, sir. I noticed that. We have been practicing fast-roping onto a very small corner of the *Okinawa*. I think we can get the team onto the deck in the upper part of the *Amuriyah*'s bow," I said, pointing to a small section of deck on the starboard side of the Iraqi vessel.

"We intercept the *Amuriyah* early tomorrow. Are the boys ready?" Coumatos asked.

"Yes, sir," I said. "I have the marines fast-roping in on the first lift, and the SEALs will be in reserve if things get sporty. All the rehearsals have gone well. We will be ready whenever you need us."

"Get some rest, Bill," Rhoads said. "Tomorrow could be an interesting day."

I thanked the commodore and the colonel, but rest was not in my plan. As the SEAL task unit commander and the senior special operations officer on the ARG, I was placed in charge of both the marine force recon and the Navy SEALs. Our mission was to board the *Amuriyah* in accordance with a United Nations resolution and stop the ship so she could be inspected for illegal cargo. In 1990, the force recon marines were the force of choice owing to their extensive maritime interdiction training. I spent the remainder of the day and into the early morning thinking through all the possible contingencies and how I would respond if the Iraqis resisted. It was time well spent.

"Assault Element to Spot One. Assault Element to Spot One!" came a blaring voice over the *Ogden*'s loudspeaker.

"Time to go, Bill," Captain Braden Phillips said, leaning back in the USS *Ogden*'s captain's chair. "Good luck," he added, smiling, as I left the bridge.

Earlier in the day, the Amphibious Task Force intercepted the *Amuriyah* in the Gulf of Oman. The ship's master was crafty. Knowing the United States wouldn't ram or try to sink the *Amuriyah*, he proceeded full speed ahead, determined that he would maintain the upper hand by refusing to stop and knowing that a 150-ton vessel plowing through the water at twenty knots is hard to stop. After several unsuccessful attempts to convince him otherwise, Coumatos ordered the boarding.

With the SEALs and the force recon embarked on the *Ogden*, I crossdecked from the *Okinawa* to the *Ogden*, did the final briefing with the operators, and stood by for the order to launch. The time was now.

Stepping out on the bridge wing of the *Ogden*, I watched as the first CH-46 helicopter lifted off from the flight deck. On board were twelve force recon marines led by marine captain Tony Stallings, call sign Wildcat. Stallings was a former defensive end from the University of Arizona, and at six foot four and 245 pounds, he was an imposing figure. Stallings and his recon marines would board the Iraqi tanker first, establish a security position, and then I would follow with another twelve marines to reinforce the element. Once we were consolidated on the ship, one element would move to the engine room, and a second element, with me and Stallings, would head to the bridge.

With my MP-5 rifle slung over my shoulder, I hurried down the starboard side ladder, across the flight deck, and onto the second helo.

"All set, sir?" the pilot asked, his voice crackling over the headset.

I glanced in the direction of First Sergeant Jack Donovan, the marine NCO in charge of my element. He looked me in the eye and gave me a thumbs-up.

"Let's go," I responded.

Seconds later, the helicopter lifted off and banked hard to the port side of the *Ogden*. Already airborne were two UH-1 Hueys with SEAL snipers aboard. I had positioned the Hueys on the port and starboard side of the *Amuriyah* to provide security overwatch during our initial fast-rope. Out the helo's side door, I could see Stallings's bird beginning its final approach on the bow of the *Amuriyah*.

On the deck of the *Amuriyah*, the ship's crew was preparing for our arrival. Water valves had been fully opened, covering the deck in several inches of water, their forceful streams blasting into the air, arching over our landing spot. Positioned near the pilot house, some members of the crew were armed with axes and pipes. But as Element One began to fast-rope onto the deck, the crew dropped their makeshift weapons and held their positions. Axes and pipes were no match for marines with guns.

Over the squad radio I could hear the SEAL snipers aboard the Hueys.

"Portside clear."

"Starboard side clear."

My radio squawked again.

"Raven. Raven. Wildcat here. Element One is onboard," came the call from Stallings.

"Roger," I responded.

Without prompting, my pilot began his approach. Below me the steel gray bow of the Iraqi tanker came into full view. Leaning out the side door, the fast-rope master tossed the heavy green rope to the deck, and one by one the marines began to exit.

"Go, go, go," yelled the rope master as I grabbed the green fast-rope and slid down the thirty feet to the deck below.

As soon as my feet touched the steel, I could see what the wily ship's master had planned for my marines. Our initial intent was to round up the crew and hold them on the mess decks until a law enforcement detachment could arrive, but immediately, the crew began to scatter. Over the ship's loudspeaker I could hear the ship's master giving orders to run and resist.

Element One headed to the engine room, but not before encountering several belligerent crewmen. After a few scuffles, which the marines seemed to enjoy, they pushed past the crew, down the interior ladders, and into the engine room.

Stallings and I headed in the opposite direction, climbing the five flights of stairs and forcing our way onto the bridge. As soon as the heavy steel door swung open, several of the ship's officers began pushing and shoving, while the master stayed on the loudspeaker yelling for his men to resist. On the decks below, dozens of crewmen were running to every corner of the tanker.

I knew from studying great military leaders that the successful ones managed to control the tempo of unfolding events by being faster with their decisions or forcing the enemy to move more slowly. Right now, the ship's master was moving faster than my ability to adjust. I needed to slow him down.

On the bridge, a phone rang, and the master picked it up.

"You have killed one of my crewmen," he screamed in broken English.

Without hesitation, I responded. "If you don't cooperate, more crewmen will die. It's your choice." It was a hollow threat that I hoped would change the dynamic on the bridge and turn the situation in my favor. It didn't.

As it turned out, a crewman had attacked First Sergeant Donovan with an axe, and Donovan knocked him out cold. No one was dead.

"You must stop your vessel now," I said calmly.

"I will not stop my ship. You are pirates!" he yelled, seething with anger.

"Either you stop your ship, or I will."

"You cannot stop my ship."

"Oh, I can, and I will," I said, moving to within

inches of his face. "My marines are in the engine room ready to shut down the engines on my order."

Several late nights of studying the *Amuriyah* and ships like her had taught me that an emergency shutdown of the engines would cause severe damage to the ship's propulsion system, like sticking a pipe in a spinning wheel.

"No! No! No!" the master shouted. "If you shut the engines down, it will destroy my ship."

This was the leverage I had been looking for, the chance to shift the tempo in my favor.

"Either you tell your men to stop resisting or I will conduct an emergency shutdown of the engines."

"You can't! You can't!" he screamed, his arms flailing about.

Turning to Stallings, I said, "Have Element One prepare for an emergency shutdown."

Out of the corner of my eye, I could see the fear on the master's face. Resisting was one thing, but having the engines on his ship ruined was quite another.

"Okay, okay, okay," he said, grabbing my arm.

Moving to the PA system, the master grabbed the microphone and instructed the crew to cooperate. Most of the crew complied, but the hardcore Iraqis continued to resist. Now that I had slowed the master's resistance, it was time to bring in the SEALs, reinforce my position, and dictate the tempo in my favor.

Over the course of the next few hours, all the crew were rounded up, the ship was brought to a slow and deliberate stop, and a law enforcement detachment was embarked. My marines and SEALs departed the *Amuriyah* and returned to the *Ogden*.

Crises have a pace and tempo all their own. Like a merciless general marching to your capital, they can force you to make bad decisions, exhaust your resources, question your leadership, and force you to react to their every move. To shift the crisis in your favor and shape the outcome, you must take the initiative and strike boldly against the most vulnerable area of the crisis. Firefighters dig firebreaks on the edges of the advancing inferno, generals attack their enemy's exposed flank, and boxers look for an opening in their rival's stance, all to slow their opponent's progress and gain the advantage. You must find opportunities, however small, that you can resolve quickly, thereby reducing the scope of the crisis and giving you the chance to make better decisions, muster your resources, and master the outcome.

In a Crisis

1. Don't try to solve all the problems at once. Identify the most vulnerable aspect of the crisis, the one you can affect the quickest.

2. Next, slow the pace of the crisis with one strong, decisive move directed at the fastest moving concern.

3. Finally, reinforce your actions with a resource-heavy approach to dictate the tempo and shape the outcome.

CHAPTER TEN

There Is Always Time for a Morale Check

You must manage your time so you can dedicate sufficient effort into maintaining the morale of your team. Without high morale, the quality of the organization's work will suffer, and your response will be less effective.

Good morale among workers is one of the greatest factors in their productivity.

—J. C. PENNEY

Austin, Texas, 2017

I stood before the podium trying to look confident. Before me were reporters from all the local papers and TV stations. They sensed blood in the water, and they knew a good downfall story was unfolding before them.

Two years earlier, in 2015, as the chancellor of the University of Texas System, I had recommended to the Board of Regents that the University of Texas System purchase 350 acres near the Texas Medical Center in Houston. They supported my recommendation, and after a year of consultation with prominent leaders around Texas, we proposed building a Texas Data Institute on the site. The idea was to build a campus that educated students from around Texas in all aspects of data science. Additionally, the campus would be a convening space for all the big companies working on artificial intelligence and machine learning. We knew the state of Texas owned a lot of data, and with the help of these companies, the institute could monetize that data to increase our endowments and lower the cost of tuition. Most folks agreed that it was a good idea, but it was a massive undertaking, and being new to Texas politics, I moved too aggressively to secure funding and dedicate resources. I also underestimated the reaction from other Texas universities, local politicians, and even some die-hard Longhorns. Most importantly, I failed to build the support necessary to galvanize the leaders in Houston and at the state capital.

Now I had to face the music. In the eyes of many, the man who had "gotten bin Laden" had also gotten too big for his britches, and in Texas, that never bodes well. I told the assembled reporters the simple truth. I had decided to cancel the project. I failed to get the support necessary, and it was time to move on. For the next thirty minutes, I answered all the questions that follow a broken promise by a public leader.

When the press conference finished, I thanked the reporters, left the room, and headed to the elevator. Each person I passed tried to avoid my gaze. In the elevator, packed with colleagues who had attended the press conference, the only sound was the soft symphony music playing in the background. After getting off the elevator, I headed to my office, smiled at my executive assistant, Kate Iannesa, and then closed the door.

The press conference had actually gone about as well as could be expected. The reporters were civil, I felt I was poised in my responses, and it ended without a lot of fanfare. Of course, by that afternoon the newspaper headlines and the television scrolls would prove more salacious than the spoken words. Earlier in the day, I had called all the relevant state senators, representatives, regents, and both the lieutenant governor and the governor. They were all courteous, but there was no mistaking their tone. I screwed up. This was a crisis of my own making that reflected poorly on me and the university system. Now I had to deal with it.

"Is he by himself?" came a booming voice from outside my office.

"Yes, sir, but I don't think this is a good time," Kate warned.

"Of course it is!"

The door swung open, and there stood Tony Cucolo, a retired Army major general now working on my staff. Tony had served as the deputy commanding general of the 10th Mountain Division in Afghanistan, commanded the 3rd Infantry Division in Iraq, and been the president of the Army War College. He had seen more combat than most general officers I knew. Tall, stocky, with broad shoulders, fading blond hair, and wearing his trademark cowboy boots, he yelled, "Morale check!"

I shot forward in my chair.

"Morale check!" he shouted again.

I couldn't help but laugh. *Morale check*. It was a familiar refrain to all of us who had served in the military. It was offered by one soldier to another when a gut punch had crushed your spirit and led to unnecessary self-pity. It was a call to man up, smile through the pain or humiliation, and get back to your job.

"Boy, you really got crushed in there. I'm glad it wasn't me. This story will surely be on the front page of the *Austin American Statesman*. No doubt Senator Smith is laughing his ass off right now." Tony smiled. "Reminds me of that time in Afghanistan when your whole team screwed up and Karzai was furious. Or that time in Iraq when your guys captured the wrong man and Petraeus was livid. How come you keep getting all these good jobs when you screw up so badly...?" My smile broadened even wider.

It was the kind of friendly harassment I needed. And then came the familiar, deep-throated laugh.

"Screw it, boss! You know you tried to do the right thing. It just didn't work out." Tony paused for a moment. "But the staff is a bit down right now…" He left the words hanging in the air.

I nodded.

"I got it, Tony."

"I know you do, boss," he said.

Tony took a few more jabs at my detractors, laughed once again, and left the room.

By that afternoon, the story was all over the local paper and even made national news. McRaven, the military hero who had commanded the mission to get bin Laden, was struggling as the chancellor. The crisis was in full view, and it reflected poorly on me and, by unfair extension, the wonderful people who worked for me.

But over the years, I had had my fair share of crises. Raids that went bad. Hostage rescues that went sideways. Air strikes that went wrong. I like to think the ledger shows I had more successes than failures, but life at the top is often punctuated with failures, and with failures come crises; crises of confidence in your leadership; reputational crises that affect your organization; legal, financial, technical, or operational crises all stemming from a failure of performance.

When these crises strike, they reflect first and foremost on the leader. And as a leader, you must move quickly to address the issue. But during a crisis, every leader needs their supporting staff to be at their best. And if, as a leader, you fail to maintain and manage the morale of your staff, you will find good advice lacking, your organizational response times slow, and your best people weighed down by fear, indecision, and self-doubt.

For the next several days, I purposely wandered the halls of the university system building. I smiled. I laughed. I talked about sports. I talked about family. I took lunch in the snack room, coffee with security personnel, and enjoyed a hoagie with the building maintenance folks. I publicly addressed the issue with my staff and assured them that I had a plan for moving forward and that everything was going to be okay.

While the issue of the failed Houston project followed me the rest of my time at the University of Texas System, the crisis was resolved quickly, morale improved, and the staff went back to serving the great people of Texas.

Napoleon once said, "An army's effectiveness depends on its size, training, experience, and morale, and morale is worth more than any of the other factors combined." No organization—no grande armée, no large corporation, no small business, and no academic institution can be successful unless the morale of the rank and file is strong. But morale is not just about being happy and content. Morale is about the effectiveness of an organization. It is about setting high standards, holding people accountable, valuing the work of your employees, and above all, showing you care about their well-being. If your employees believe that they are nothing more than a material asset, a resource, a bargaining chip, or another cog in the business wheel, then at a critical point, when you need them the most, you may find their morale is not sufficient to get you through the crisis. This aspect of crisis leadership requires careful time management, personnel management, and resource management. As a leader, you must always show your troops, your employees, your workers, that they matter—particularly during a crisis.

In a Crisis

1. Spend time with the rank and file during a crisis. They are looking for your guidance and your inspiration. If their morale is high, you will get through the crisis much more quickly.

2. Appearances matter. In a public forum, always look confident. But it's a crisis for a reason, and maybe that reason is you—so be equally gracious and humble.

3. Your morale matters. Have someone you trust who can boost your spirits when disaster strikes; someone who can help you manage your physical well-being and your mental toughness, and who can maintain your sense of humor.

CONCLUSION

In his 2014 novel *The Martian*, author Andy Weir tells the story of astronaut Mark Watney, who gets marooned on the Red Planet after his crew, believing he was killed in a solar storm, leaves him behind. As the storm subsides and Watney regains consciousness, he finds himself alone. Realizing that he is stranded on Mars, the first step he takes is to *assess* his situation. How much food and water does he have? How much air? Is there a way to communicate with NASA? Can he survive until the next Mars mission arrives? Watney is in the midst of a true crisis. He must know, unequivocally, whether he has the resources to survive. He must do a thorough assessment.

Back on planet Earth, a memorial service is held for Watney, and the entire world mourns his death. Then, two months later, an analyst comes to believe

Watney has survived. The first report of Watney's death was clearly in error. Now *NASA* must assess the situation. Is it really Watney? Is the analyst correct? If it is Watney, can he survive much longer? The administrator calls together his close advisors to get recommendations on how to proceed. Eventually, the analyst's report is confirmed, but now the NASA administrator must decide whether, after the global outpouring of love and support, he should *report* to the press that Watney is alive. After some heated discussions, NASA realizes they have no choice. As embarrassing and as gut-wrenching as it is, NASA must report to the world that they left Mark Watney on Mars.

The novel takes on a brisk pace as NASA and an international team of scientists and engineers respond quickly to *contain* the crisis and hopefully bring Watney home. They look at all their options and eventually put all of them into play, including reaching out to the Chinese for a backup rocket. On Mars, Watney is also reviewing his options and making some bold decisions on what steps he must take to survive and hopefully return to Earth. Unless he takes decisive steps, the situation is going to get worse. Doing nothing is not an option.

At NASA, the rescue coordinator is *shaping* the outcome of the crisis by micromanaging every aspect of the mission, from public relations to the engineering solutions. There is no room for error or haphazard work. Eventually, Watney and NASA develop a manageable rescue plan. Watney will drive across Mars, locate an old Mars ascent vehicle (MAV), strip it of all its excess weight, and launch back into orbit. The Ares 3 crew, who has turned around their starship to rescue Watney, will conduct a precarious rendezvous in orbit to try to capture Mark as he spirals through space. Throughout the entire novel, and later in the movie starring Matt Damon, Watney's crew from the Ares 3 works to maintain Watney's sense of humor and morale. It is this aspect of the story that so endears the characters to the readers.

In classic Hollywood fashion, the rendezvous in space is filled with perilous moments, where Watney barely makes the linkup but somehow manages to survive and returns to Earth a hero. Fiction is often a great place to learn about the fundamentals of surviving a crisis. The writers can create the worst-case scenario and then weave the perfect narrative to show the audience how the heroes navigate the challenges and come out victorious. Real life, of course, is much more complicated, nuanced, and fraught with unpredictable human interaction, but having an intellectual model for understanding the right steps to take is still valuable.

When a crisis hits, every leader must first *assess the situation* to get a basic understanding of the effect the crisis is having on their organization. Both the fictional NASA of *The Martian* and the real NASA of Apollo 13 began by getting all the facts they could muster. In the military, every commander has a commander's critical information requirement (CCIR). The CCIR is generally provided to the junior officer on watch who has the responsibility to "wake up the boss" when things get bad. The CCIRs include catastrophic events like a soldier being injured or killed, major damage to equipment, an environmental accident, or serious malfeasance on the part of a C-suite employee. Basically, you wake up the boss if you think an event will make the front page of the *Washington Post*, the *New York Times*, or any major publication. Every organization needs some reporting criteria that trigger a corporate crisis response team. These criteria are the basis for your initial assessment and therefore should be as detailed as possible.

Next comes the *reporting phase*. Mark Twain

was quoted as saying, "A lie can travel halfway around the world before the truth is putting on its shoes." Charles Kingsley, a British clergyman and writer from about the same era, put it more succinctly when he said, "Misinformation is more dangerous than no information at all."

Looking across history, initial misinformation about a catastrophic event is much more prevalent than the truth.

- In 1912, the *Titanic* set sail from Southampton, England, bound for New York City. On April 14, four days out from England, she struck an iceberg. Initial reports stated that the ship was okay and being towed to port with all passengers safe aboard. The passengers were anything but safe. Two hours later, more than 1,500 of them perished as the ship went down.
- On December 7, 1941, messages came in from Hawaii describing the Japanese attack on Pearl Harbor. Initial reports suggested minor damage to the fleet. By the time the attack was over, 2,400 Americans were dead and the entire armada of American battleships were sunk.

- As President John Kennedy waited anxiously for the first reports from Cuba on April 18, 1962, he was told that the invasion by Cuban freedom fighters at the Bay of Pigs was making significant progress against Castro's communist forces. But, in fact, the landing had been an unmitigated disaster, and during three days of fighting, more than 120 Cuban exiles were killed in the battle and hundreds more captured and executed.
- As the US embassy in Tehran came under attack on November 4, 1979, President Jimmy Carter was assured that the situation was under control and that the hostages would be released soon. The public was told that the students were only there for a symbolic occupation. But it wasn't until four hundred forty-four days later, after a failed hostage rescue attempt and a US president was out of office, that the hostages finally returned home.
- One of the more damning failures of first reports came on August 29, 2005, when the good people of New Orleans and those along the US Gulf Coast were told by the news that Hurricane Katrina had weakened significantly

and "we dodged a bullet." Within twenty-four hours, the massive rains overwhelmed the levee system and in time more than 80 percent of New Orleans was underwater.

First reports are almost always in error. Not because the people closest to the event are bad people, but with crisis come confusion, trauma, and panic, and therefore a leader should be skeptical of all first reports. Always be prepared to react to the worst-case scenario. Then and only then will you have marshaled the resources necessary to contain the crisis. If you underappreciate the danger of unfolding events, you could be in for a surprise. But, of course, it's not only the incoming reports that are crucial; it's how you, as a leader, report the evolving crisis that may determine the success or failure of your organization.

If a crisis is developing, it generally means that something your organization did or failed to do is responsible. It's a painful truth, but history is replete with examples:

- A gas leak at the Union Carbide plant in Bhopal, India, in 1984 resulted in the deaths of 3,000 people. The leak was a product of poor maintenance, inadequate safety standards, and corporate negligence.

- The Enron scandal (2001) that caused the collapse of an American energy company was due to widespread corporate fraud and corruption.
- The *Deepwater Horizon* oil spill (2010) that resulted in one of the largest environmental disasters in history was caused by cost-cutting measures that affected rig safety.
- The Volkswagen emissions scandal (2015) involved company leadership deliberately manipulating emissions tests.
- The Theranos biotech company's (2018) revolutionary blood-testing technology turned out to be a scam.
- Most recently, the Boeing 737 Max aircraft crashes (2018–2019) that killed 346 people resulted from poor design and inadequate safety measures.

In almost every case, the companies waited before notifying the public of the crisis. Unscrupulous or imprudent leaders hoped, in vain, that their misdeeds might go unnoticed, or the blame for the crisis could be shifted elsewhere. Assuming that you are one of the good leaders, report the bad news as quickly, as accurately, and as fully as you possibly can. The sooner your bosses and the public are aware of the problem, the sooner you can begin to address the underlying causes. Even amid a tragedy, the public will keep its trust in you—if you are honest. Remember the old saying, "the truth always finds a way to surface, no matter how deep in the darkness it has been buried."

Once you have assessed the problem and reported it up the chain, it's time to respond. Just like the second law of thermodynamics, the crisis won't get better on its own. You must first take action to slow the momentum (*contain*) and then turn that momentum in your favor (*shape*).

Nothing is more of a crisis than getting caught in a real combat ambush where your life and the lives of your troops are at risk. During basic SEAL training, our instructors taught us the fundamentals of escaping an ambush. First, you must assess the situation, albeit quickly, and almost simultaneously, you must report to the SEALs in the platoon which direction you intend the unit to move. Then you must act immediately, with greater force than the enemy. For SEALs caught in an ambush, this means everyone in the platoon turning toward the enemy and firing their weapons on full automatic. While this combat tactic may seem like a strange analogy for dealing with an organizational crisis, the lesson is simple. You must find a way to counter the momentum of the crisis by allocating as many resources as possible (manpower, equipment, money) as quickly as possible to the crisis's most accessible or vulnerable site.

Firefighters attempting to slow a fast-moving forest fire will begin by attacking the edge of the fire with everything they can bring to bear. They will dig trenches, conduct controlled burns, and create firebreaks all to slow the fire's momentum. Once they have slowed the fire's spread, then they can attack the fire directly.

Frequently, when confronted with a crisis, leaders will parse out organizational resources in hopes of saving money, saving executives' time, or saving capital resources. But when calamity strikes, being parsimonious will only prolong the crisis.

Sometimes the hardest part of a crisis is the *management phase*. When the adrenaline wears off, when the exhaustion sets in, when the momentum has swung in your favor, organizations tend to get complacent. The real threat is over, or so they believe.

This is the time when the management aspect of being a leader is so crucial.

In March of 2020, I was the keynote speaker at the Navy SEAL Foundation gala in New York City. There were 2,000 attendees, and during the pre-dinner reception, there was a smattering of talk about this new virus that was going around. Within a week, the COVID-19 pandemic was all anyone could talk about. But some experts believed that with swift global action, lockdowns, testing, and contact tracing, the spread of the virus could be contained within a few months. The SARS outbreak in 2002 and the H1N1 outbreak in 2009 were both contained quite quickly. Most Americans thought we would be finished with the pandemic by the summer of 2020. It was eighteen months before a vaccine was developed, and more than two years later, May 11, 2023, before the US government declared the end of the COVID-19 public health emergency.

The two years of the pandemic required the government, hospitals, schools, public and private companies, and the average citizen to manage the crisis long-term. Not since the Great Depression of 1929 had America confronted such an enduring disruption in daily activity. In January of 2020, a COVID task force was established. The task force quickly issued travel restrictions and stay-at-home orders, invoked the Defense Production Act to increase the critical supplies of personal protective equipment (PPE) and expanded testing and contact tracing. By May 2020 the task force launched Operation Warp Speed. But the virus continued to spread, and hopes of quelling the pandemic by the summer vanished.

As the crisis continued, all elements of federal, state, and local government as well as corporate America settled in for the long haul. The federal government issued economic relief packages to provide financial support to businesses, families, and individuals. The Centers for Disease Control (CDC) provided daily updates on the status of the virus and preventive measures. Guidelines were promulgated concerning mask mandates and social distancing. Across the country, Americans moved to virtual meetings and worked from home. They also needed and received expanded home delivery services. By year's end, we had a vaccine, and immunization sites could be found at every hospital, school gym, and local church.

While there will be endless debate about the nature of the pandemic and the merits of actions taken, the steps to finally end the crisis were methodical, deliberate, and time consuming. I, for one, will always be thankful and in awe of those biotech workers, scientists, researchers, teachers, and civil servants who brought America and the world back from the edge of disaster. Those dedicated public servants, heroic health care workers, fearless delivery people, and office workers all had to manage the crisis so they could go about their daily lives—even if it was drastically different than before the pandemic.

Most crises won't last two years, but whether it's years, months, weeks, or days, after the initial response, a leader must be prepared to manage the workforce and the resources until the final resolution. This aspect of crisis leadership can often be the most challenging.

San Antonio, Texas, 1970

To an outsider, Friday afternoon, April 17, 1970, at Roosevelt High School looked like any other day. The spring temperature hovered around the mid-seventies, students hurried to their classes between the bells, teachers patrolled the hallways; the weekend was just three hours away. But April 17 in San Antonio was unlike any other day most of us teenagers had ever experienced. The student population of Roosevelt High School was predominantly children of military families; fathers who had served in World War II, Korea, or Vietnam. Children who were raised by the Greatest Generation to appreciate American exceptionalism, to proudly stand for the flag, to say the Pledge of Allegiance, and to honor those service men and women who sacrificed for the nation. We were a patriotic bunch, and as the televisions were wheeled into our classrooms, we all watched, transfixed on the news that was unfolding in front of us.

On the television the reporter said, "We are now looking at the last moments of Apollo 13. The best we can do now is to listen and hope." Black-and-white images of sailors aboard the USS *Iwo Jima* filled the tiny screen. The countdown clock read 1:20 minutes to reentry. Then came the report, "Houston, we have lost communications." I looked around the classroom, and some of the girls and the boys were quietly crying. The reporter anxiously let the audience know that the capsule was coming in faster than expected, "faster than any spacecraft had returned from space before." The classroom was dead quiet. We all understood that threes lives hung in the balance, and we worried that if this recovery mission failed, maybe America wasn't as exceptional as we had been told. The reporters' faces flashed on the screen, mirroring our collective fear. At NASA, engineers, astronauts, and some family members stood nervously listening and watching for any sign of the capsule carrying Lovell, Haise, and Swigert. Back in the Pacific, a helicopter hovered over a bare patch of ocean hoping to see three parachutes carrying our American heroes. Suddenly, a voice penetrated the airwaves: "Odyssey, this is Houston, how do you read?" "Okay, Joe," came the response from Jim Swigert in the command module. Moments later the crowd at Mission Control erupted in cheers. "There they are! They made it!" In our small classroom at Roosevelt High School, our pride in America had never been greater. The biggest crisis in our young lives had ended in success.

At approximately 1:07 p.m. Eastern Standard Time on April 17, 1970, the command module Odyssey, carrying the three Apollo 13 astronauts, splashed down in the South Pacific. Helicopters from the USS *Iwo Jima* hovered overhead as Lovell, Haise, and Swigert exited the capsule. Moments later, they were hoisted aboard the helicopters and flown back to the ship. On the USS *Iwo Jima*, hundreds of sailors clapped, shouted, and cheered loudly as the three men exited the helos. Around the world, celebrations broke out. Millions of people, from all nations, all walks of life, from every corner of the world, were thankful for the astronauts' return. The safe return of the three men was hailed as one of NASA's finest moments. The NASA team followed every phase of crisis resolution, from assessing and reporting, to containing, shaping, and managing. The engineers, the ground controllers, fellow Earthbound astronauts, the administrators, and, above all, Mission Control turned a crisis into a crowning moment of achievement.

A few days after returning home, Captain Jim Lovell spoke to the press. He showered praise on the entire NASA team and said, "NASA's response to the crisis was a perfect example of how preparation, training, and ingenuity can overcome even the most dire situations."

I hope the lessons of *Conquering Crisis* will provide you the tools you need to overcome any dire situation and return your organization safely home with the admiration and respect of your workforce, your stakeholders, and the public.

ACKNOWLEDGMENTS

I would like to thank my son Major Bill McRaven, USAF (Retired), for his words of wisdom and insight that helped me frame the idea behind *Conquering Crisis*. Additionally, I am incredibly thankful to my new editor, Colin Dickerman, for his patience and professionalism and to the Hachette team of Melanie Gold and Ian Dorset. Finally, none of my books would ever become a reality without the guidance and friendship of Bob Barnett. I am forever in your debt.

ABOUT THE AUTHOR

Admiral William H. McRaven (US Navy, Retired) is the #1 *New York Times* bestselling author of *Make Your Bed* and *The Wisdom of the Bullfrog* and the *New York Times* bestsellers *Sea Stories: My Life in Special Operations* and *The Hero Code: Lessons Learned from Lives Well Lived*. In his thirty-seven years as a Navy SEAL, he commanded at every level. As a Four-Star Admiral, his final assignment was as Commander of all US Special Operations Forces. After retiring from the Navy, he served as the Chancellor of the University of Texas System from 2015 to 2018. He now lives in Austin, Texas, with his wife, Georgeann.